It's Okay to Miss the Bed on the First Jump

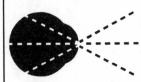

This Large Print Book carries the
Seal of Approval of N.A.V.H.

It's Okay to Miss the Bed on the First Jump

AND OTHER LIFE LESSONS I LEARNED FROM DOGS

John O'Hurley

THORNDIKE PRESS

An imprint of Thomson Gale, a part of The Thomson Corporation

Detroit • New York • San Francisco • New Haven, Conn. • Waterville, Maine • London

THOMSON

GALE

™

LIBRARY OF CONGRESS CATALOGING-IN-PUBLICATION DATA

O'Hurley, John.
  It's okay to miss the bed on the first jump : and other life lessons I learned from dogs / by John O'Hurley. — Large print ed.
    p. cm.
  ISBN-13: 978-0-7862-9485-5 (hardcover : alk. paper)
  ISBN-10: 0-7862-9485-X (hardcover : alk. paper)
  1. O'Hurley, John. 2. Dogs — United States — Anecdotes. 3. Dog owners — United States — Biography. 4. Human-animal relationships — United States — Anecdotes. 5. Conduct of life — Anecdotes. I. Title.
SF426.2.O35 2007
636.7—dc22   2007000360

Published in 2007 by arrangement with Hudson Street Press, a member of Penguin Group (USA) Inc.

Printed in the United States of America on permanent paper
10 9 8 7 6 5 4 3 2 1

To my parents, who among all the opportunities they gave me, first brought a dog into my life.
To my wife, Lisa, who has shown our dogs and me a depth of love we have never known and has given me a deeper understanding of why they like her better than me.

CONTENTS

I begin with a conclusion.

My life is richer for the presence of my dogs. Not just my dogs alone, but all the dogs that have slept in my lap, run across fields where I've played with them, or leaned out car windows as I've driven by. I have fed them, held them, massaged their necks, rubbed their bellies, and thrown them sticks and toys as far as my arm could reach. They have chased me, caught me, and licked me until I had to surrender. I have grown up with them and watched them grow with me, and I've sadly watched some pass on. On occasion, I have helped to heal them, and more often, they have helped to heal me. I have taught them things of some importance: how to sit, how to shake hands, and how to roll over. In turn, they have taught me to believe in the constant goodness that seems to emanate so easily from their gentle and loving nature. They are the dogs of my life.

When I was a senior in high school, I wrote a poem as a way to explore both my newfound fascination with language and my newly formed swirl of teenage hormones. It was pretty unmemorable work, save for one particular line:

> I am of those I've touched, and the best of what they are.

That is probably the most prophetic I have ever been on my own behalf. Over the years, if I have developed any sense of virtue for my own life, it is because I was lucky enough to have seen and embraced the examples of greatness all around me — from my parents, my wife, my family, my friends, and, yes, my dogs.

As humans, we tend to expose our goodness in glimpses. Dogs, however, live closer to their essence, and they are more constant in their goodness. Perhaps that is why God gives them to us — as teachers, to stay by our sides in quiet vigil, undisturbed by worry or regret, and to show us how to live each moment as it comes.

I am a much better person with a dog in my lap.

Precious Gifts Come in Small Packages

At five, I was convinced that the answer to every important question was found at a pond. And not just any pond. You couldn't just happen upon any quiet body of water and expect to walk away with some sort of epiphany. It had to be my pond. The one at the end of the street, deep in the New England woods, a few hundred yards from our house in Natick, Massachusetts.

It was quiet and embraceable. I could map every path around it in my head, although some parts weren't navigable by a five-year-old and I'd only heard about those. There was a high point of rock from which I could see most of the world. There were railroad tracks on the far end where occasionally the world would pass me by on its way to somewhere else. Lush green in spring and summer, on fire in the fall, and sparse gray in the winter freeze, the pond was always a special place. On this point Thoreau and I have always agreed. He went to his pond to live deliberately, and I went to mine to deliberate.

I had a lot of questions then that required contemplation. Five was a busy year for me. I was on the young end of the class starting first grade that year and I was a bit overwhelmed by the responsibilities. I was left-handed so I wrote from right to left across the page. My numbers were backward, too, so the teacher would have to correct my arithmetic papers in the mirror. I had a small head and ears that stuck out a bit like two chunks of cauliflower on a very small globe, which concerned me. This look was only aggravated by the Parris Island butch haircut that my parents seemed to find so fashionable.

There was also a girl in our first grade class, a bit diminutive in height with buck teeth and profoundly hairy legs. The seemingly inborn cruelty of five- and six-year-olds made them swarm to her like the wild dogs of Moremi around an emotional kill. I was always torn between the need to participate with the crowd and my empathy for her loneliness.

But there was another particularly poignant problem brewing for me. The class was a pretty unruly one, even for kids of such a young age. When the teacher left the room on her break, as teachers did back then, the class was left alone in the room with the instructions to work quietly at our desks and not to make a sound or we'd all have to stay after school. I would tie my hands into a blood knot and pray to what little I understood of God that everyone would be quiet just this once. Staying after school meant missing the bus. Missing the school bus was like falling off the edge of the earth because I wasn't sure how I would get home. I wasn't even sure where I lived. And if I couldn't get home, where would I eat?

Inevitably, the teacher would return to a classroom that looked like the evacuation of Saigon. The girl with the hairy legs was still working quietly at her desk, while I was slumped over mine with my head buried in my arms — to make it crystal clear to the teacher that I had been even quieter than quiet. I was almost asleep and really, really, really innocent of the mayhem around me. It didn't matter — it was punishment for one and punishment for all. We would have to stay after school, and I would never see my family or my dog again. In my mind it was case-closed. The injustice of the moment was too much for me to bear. I burst

15

out in tears loud enough for all to hear, loud enough even for the little girl with the hairy legs to feel sorry for me.

The five minutes the teacher kept us in our seats in silence after the bell rang passed drip by drip. I split my focus between the firmness of her stare and the presence of the yellow bus out the window, almost full. Finally, she said, "Class dismissed," but I heard, "Go ye to live another day."

The school bus waited, the guilty and the not guilty loaded on, and I made it home. But I figured this was just a one-time reprieve, so every day when the teacher left for her coffee and a smoke I would plead with the rank and file for quiet, which only served to fan the flames of misconduct. The teacher returned, I would cry, we would stay after school. In fact, one of the kids actually told me that most of the kids talked because they liked to see me cry. This was pretty much the cycle of first grade, and my first taste of social inequity.

So there was a lot to reflect upon at the pond. There I would write songs in my head and an occasional poem, but mostly I would just wonder about things and try to catch turtles. My mother later remarked that one of the neighborhood mothers said I was always so sad. I wasn't sad. I was always thinking and trying to catch turtles.

And I was never alone. It was on these paths that I would walk for hours after school and all weekend long with Taffy, a dachshund and my first dog. I always thought Taffy was built a little funny. Short, spindly legs and a long, chestnut packing tube of a body gave her a kind of brisk, side-to-side saunter as she quietly followed behind me, never questioning my route and never missing the meaning of every moment. I would ask her questions while I sat on the rocky point that leaned out over the pond. Questions like, if I was supposed to be an actor, which I knew I was — that lightbulb went off in my head at three — then why wasn't I picked for a speaking part in the class skit, "Four and Twenty Blackbirds"?

Taffy could always tell when I was asking her a question. She would tilt her head slightly as if it allowed her to grasp my dilemma better. Then she'd quietly stare without blinking for just long enough to show that she cared. She wasn't able to give me the answer, which was that the teacher picked the cast with speaking parts from the top reading group, while I was still trying to figure out which side of the page to start from. But the answer wasn't important.

I became an actor in spite of that momentary setback, although I still find myself humming that nursery rhyme from time to time, half wondering if it impacted my career. Perhaps that will always be my *Hamlet.*

No matter now, Taffy was teaching me through silence and companionship that problems and disappointments lose their power when they're put into words. It was a good lesson to learn young that answers are not always important; they will come. When we verbalize a worry, we remove it from our imagination, where it can grow and fester and do us the most harm. So I would talk to Taffy as much as she would listen.

Despite her unassuming wisdom, she could never seem to get out of her own way. Taffy got into trouble a lot. Most of the time it wasn't her fault. Most of the time it involved a skunk of some sort. The woods around the pond were filled with them, and Taffy was as curious as she was defensive of her turf. She was a sucker for a skunk, and in the summer, it seemed almost once a month that my father was marinating her in tomato juice to cut the smell from her latest douse of curiosity.

The skunk was a perplexing creature to me, even at five. I was told in school that everything had a purpose, but for the life of me I couldn't figure out what purpose was served by a skunk in the many plateaus of life. And as I have grown older, I still can't imagine what part of the food chain would be greatly upset if we removed them altogether.

To make matters worse, God seemed to have compounded this mistake by replicating it as vegetation. The woods around the pond were quilted with a large, green, leafy cluster called skunk cabbage, which also smelled like its mammalian counterpart when attacked by the heel of a shoe. Now, Taffy saw everything from an altitude of ten inches, except on those occasions when I would pick her up and give her a rarified view of the world from my height. As I would beat down the path in front of me, inevitably I would clip off a leaf of skunk cabbage, Taffy would get the drippings, and my father would once again have to make her part of a large, galvanized Bloody Mary.

Taffy left the house one day in the company of my father after she bit the mailman, and didn't return. It really crushed me. I remember walking down by the pond, realizing she wasn't going to be there anymore. I didn't get much of an explanation from my parents, except that biting mailmen was wrong. To date, I have never bitten one. I guess Taffy taught me that, too.

We moved after first grade to another state, so I lost the pond, too. I have thought of Taffy and the pond, now inseparable in memory, often over the many years. I think of how fortunate I was to have both a companion and a space at one of those pivotal points in one's personal story. It was a time when I was filled with wonder and struggle to make sense of circumstances and first-time feelings. It was a time when it was easy to become your circumstances, as I did with my buried head on a first grade desk. It was also a time that exposed me to several great life lessons.

I recall Taffy's doe-eyed look as I talked to her about all manner of things and I learned that the gift is in the listening, not the answering. I learned not to empower a problem by silence but to put it out there in the world with words. And, as I would take a half-look over my shoulder to see her picking her way through the skunk cabbage, pausing only briefly for a significant smell, I learned from Taffy that every journey has a reason, and to pause often enough to not miss the meaning of every moment.

To this day, I hope the same for the girl

with the hairy legs.

I have had several dogs since Taffy and have two presently. As I write this, two sets of eyes are staring me down. The black one is Betty, a stray from the Hollywood Hills, rescued six years ago. She is actually a dachshund/black Lab mix — if you can imagine anything as painful as that. I'm guessing Mom was just a very slow dachshund — or, if it was the dad, it was the luckiest leap he ever made. But she is a happy mix, resembling a Lab puppy both in her size and energy. Betty was frail, shell-shocked, and bearded — yes, bearded — when she was rescued. No one knows how many weeks or months she spent hiding from the coyotes. Today I suspect she reflects the simple joy for life of any creature that has been near death. She stares at me now, waiting for any indication that I might leave the chair or the room. She would then pick up in an instant and follow, as if to reassure me that anything I wanted to do would be much more interesting than her plans.

Then there is Scoshi, a little white Maltese with an alpha personality that age is starting to quell. He has been everywhere with me. His stare is mostly a squint now.

Another nap is on its way, and as long as I sit in this chair and write, I'm moving at his speed.

I think because I've been in the company of dogs my whole life and because I'm still in wonder at life's simple truths, I find the two are inseparable. I've had other pets. I was preoccupied with the turtles in the pond and the toads in the woods. But turtles teach you little. And if a five-year-old can catch them, they are not really in a position to mentor much anyway.

I do remember on one particular trip to the pond catching twenty-seven toads in an afternoon. This was long before I was aware that, by catching and keeping them, I might be tipping the delicate balance of nature. I kept them in a box under the stairs of the house by the driveway. Apparently, instead of trying to jump out individually, they planned their escape en masse but, unfortunately, at just the same time my mother was pulling our '59 Chevy into the driveway, and what followed was something of a massacre. I learned absolutely nothing from them.

Then I had horned toads, guinea pigs, chameleons, goldfish, mice, more mice, and finally a teenage obsession with horses. Say what you will about the bond between horse and owner, but even a horse lover will admit that if you were attacked, your dog would be the first to come to your defense — even Scoshi would disturb his nap long enough to help me out with a bite or two. That is, as long as it wasn't a mailman — they're still off-limits.

The loyalty of a dog is cliché, but a dog's ability to bring meaning to life, both funny and deep, is only limited by the length of their lives and appreciable only to those who take the time to observe them. I have found many truths that exist in parallel between our lives and theirs. (Every person with a dog in their life seems to have a personal story to support that notion.) I offer mine here as poignantly and humorously as they have affected me. It's my way of sharing the wonderful experience of Taffy, Betty, Scoshi, and all the dogs in between, and not missing the meaning they bring.

WHEN A DOG BARKS
— LISTEN

I was recently doing a voice-over for "Star Johnson," a character that I play in the animated television series *Duck Dodgers*. At one point, the script called for my character to bark like a dog. When it came time for the bark, I leaned toward the microphone, pursed my lips together, and made the requisite "woof" sound. I could see the director through a wall of glass sitting in the control booth. She was fairly unimpressed and asked me to try another take.

"WOOF!" I barked again.

My voice was louder, but the bark wasn't any better. I did take after take until another actor at the recording session quietly interrupted to explain that a dog's bark is mimicked by inhaling the "woof" into the abdomen, not by exhaling the breath through the mouth. This had never occurred to me. It was fascinating. I tried his method and sure enough, I could bark. To this day I can fool any dog with its authenticity. My bark — and the fascinating science behind it — is now a precious piece of trivia I dish out when the conversation dips at a cocktail party.

The simple fact that I find a dog bark fascinating probably invalidates any other observations I could ever make, but there is something both interesting and instructive in what is truly one of nature's great annoyances — The Bark.

What is equally odd is that it took me four days in a car with Scoshi to find the message and the meaning.

It seemed, on the surface, like the perfect novelistic experience — traveling cross-country, New York to L.A., with nothing more than a convertible sports car, a road map, and my dog. A kind of Damon Runyon brush with the uncommon romance of living moment to moment, rest stop to rest stop. A chance to bond with my dog as the hum of the tires on the wet pavement rocked him gently to sleep on the bucket seat next to me. Then my mind would drift off — at first to the quiet of the moment, then to the meaning of the journey, and finally to the meaning of meaning, which, of course, made no sense at all. But it was a chance for a rare few days to live poetically

— just man, map, and dog. And so it was that night in 1994, as we headed out across the George Washington Bridge, the rain pelting the windshield in a fitting act of ambience. It was equally appropriate that the journey began at night, for there is nothing like darkness to sharpen the senses.

The trip marked the beginning of the breakup of my first marriage, so it was not the happiest of times. The melancholy of the moment made me appreciate what I had, what I was losing, and the inestimable value of the bond with the little white body quietly snoring next to me.

Scoshi was presented to me as a gift from my first wife prior to our engagement, some three years earlier. He was only six weeks old when I first held him, a tiny flurry of licks and nibbles that barely took up the space of my palm. The name, Scoshi, came appropriately as an anglicized version of the Japanese word *sukoshi,* meaning "a little bit." He has little black button eyes and nose, and puppy-cut short, white hair. He always reminds me of a little, bearded coal miner in white long johns, an image that I have shared with others from time to time, amusing only me, apparently. Scoshi also has the most interesting habit of tilting his head from side to side when asked even the

simplest of questions, as though he under-
stands everything except the last word and
is trying to work it out. This look of constant
wonder makes him appear as though a trick
cigar just blew up in his face.

I knew instantly that Scoshi was *my* dog. I
quickly taught him to shake with either paw,
lie down, roll over, and circle-dance on two
legs at dinnertime. He would let me flip him
on his back and stroke his belly while I held
him like a baby. I could grab his two front
paws and send him flying on his back across
the hardwood floors. I still don't know what
possessed me to first try that, but he was
game for it every time. We had a direct line
of communication, expressed best by the
soulful nature of his constant stare. He
would tilt his head and listen, listen and tilt.
It was what I needed most on that long
journey.

Make no mistake about it, Scoshi is also
an alpha male, and more important to the
tale, a barker who protects his turf. It's a
kind of piercing tenor that endears him to
no one, once he gets hold of a good reason
to fire off a volley. Once he'd done his bonding with one human, that was enough. All
others beware.

He directed most of his hostility toward
his own kind. To any dog that crossed his

path, it was a kind of bite-first, greet-later how d'ya do. But all of that belies the calm of the moment in the car that dark night. His eyes knit shut, and his little pink belly rising and falling in a rhythm with the wipers. The little snores coming in cadence in a quiet kind of late-night jazz as we cut our path to California.

The excitement of the journey seemed to temporarily quell many of the feelings I'd had about the circumstances of my life at that time. The adventure gave me a temporary sense of resilience that was enough to keep me awake well into the night. I stopped at the occasional truck stop to sample the coffee and to briefly participate in the world of the all-night trucker. I read the trucker magazines and leafed through pages of trucking opportunities in the trucker classified ads as I sat in diner booths. I ate trucker food, which meant adding steak to my eggs. I even walked Scoshi through the endless sea of cabs and trailers moored for the night in the lot and let him lift his leg to mark his own little place against the wheels of these giants. They became familiar ships in the night, them passing us and us passing them on the interstate. It was as though we had all caught the crest of the same wave headed west, where they would unload their cargo, and Scoshi and I would begin the next chapter of our lives.

We were nearly twenty-four hours into the trip when we made our first attempt to stop for the night. Scoshi had slept in every position possible in the car. In the front seat, in the backseat, he even wedged himself between my neck and the headrest and slept with his face pressed against the window. Occasionally he would wake to climb up onto the console of the car, sit down, and just stare at me. I know this stare so well. It's a stare with so many meanings. This time it was saying, "Dad, can you and I change seats?"

I actually let Scoshi drive for a while. It was on a ridiculously straight stretch of highway outside Amarillo, Texas. It was a pretty stretch of road, if you find beauty in starkness. I put him in my lap and placed his front paws on either side of the steering wheel. He stood up on his hind legs, and his natural sense of balance held the car in line for the better part of twenty minutes. I stroked his back while he drove. It was a fair deal by anyone's standards. I also leaned my seat back so that my head was hidden by the partition between the front and rear windows. As cars passed and the drivers casually glanced over at us, they would double-take at the little white-bearded man in long johns driving a late-model sports car.

But then it was time to rest. No-tell hotels and motels lined the interstate that cut through Amarillo. There were billboards above each one with the price of a room and the promise of a better night's rest. I started playing poker with the prices: $15.95 a night . . . $14.95 a night . . . $13.50 a night . . . and finally $12.95. Yes, a full night's sleep for two for only $12.95.

The thick, yellowed Plexiglas window separated me from the night manager and his nap. He was a slightly unkempt Woody Allen type, if Woody had ever committed to faded western wear. He was slightly startled when I tapped on the window with my keys to inquire about a room for the night. Apparently it had been a while since anyone had checked in. The front parking lot was pretty much empty.

Scoshi was still in the car out of view, which turned out to be a good thing. There was a small sign on the window with large, bold, capital letters that read ABSOLUTELY NO PETS. This, of course, was much stronger language than simply NO PETS, and it indicated that someone had crossed this path before. Just under that was an equally venomous cartoon of a dog in a circle with a red line through it. This apparently was the universal symbol for the large throng of international visitors that came to this lovely hovel strictly to test the strength of the previous warning. Woody made me prepay the whole $12.95 before handing me the key.

Our room was around the back of the motel complex, so I drove with one hand on the wheel and one over Scoshi's mouth, lest he start barking to warn anyone within earshot that we were camping here for the night. There were a dozen cars parked out back, which made me realize that we were not alone. We found a spot right in front of our room. Apparently Woody Allen was stuffing the place from back to front that night, an executive decision that bewildered me, and one that I was too tired to grasp.

I barely had a chance to experience all sixty watts of overhead illumination before Scoshi started to shoot around the room, corner to corner, measuring the foreign soil that he would now have to defend. He disappeared into the bathroom, which was the size of an afterthought, and quickly returned. He jumped up and began a nasal exam of the bed, which was large enough for my frame, but had a distinct and definite slope to the center, perhaps for drainage purposes. Scoshi tore through the pillows, upending each one and rolling on them all to give them the benefit of his scent. When he finished he stood up and looked straight at me, hair all tousled, like a rag doll that had been loved a bit too much. Then he tilted his head to me to say, "Okay, Dad, the place is safe."

I left him on the bed briefly to shower up. As I unwrapped the slice of complimentary soap, which was just small enough to discourage you from taking any leftover with you, I noticed that the shower water held a curious tint that reminded me of the amber flow of the River Ganges. It gave me that all-over clean feeling you get from river-laundering with the fishwives of New Delhi. The towel was large enough so that, in the event of fire and I needed to run screaming from the room, I could cover my front or my back, but not both. And in the most fitting touch of irony, the small paper bath mat on which I was standing featured the words "Thank You" in flowing script. These are the extra touches you expect when you decide to open the wallet and break the ten-dollar mark.

I pulled the blanket and top sheet back and climbed into the canoe. The sheets felt like the itchy wool of my gray flannel slacks in Catholic school. I tried to lie perfectly still, knowing that if I tossed and turned all night the nap of the sheets would rip the hair off my legs. Scoshi settled in, mimicking my position and spooning up to me with his head on the pillow, just as my wife used to do. Now that she was gone, it was as if he knew that he would have to take her place. Dogs just have that instinct. The sense of loss and the gentleness of this little gesture made me weep for the first time since we'd left New York.

The privacy of the moment, however, evaporated as soon as I turned out the light. The couple in the room next door was apparently watching television and couldn't agree on a channel. Their argument then grew to explore other areas of their marital discontent, and pretty soon we had ourselves a full-voiced spat. Having spent all the money on the apparent bathroom appointments, this fine establishment had nothing left in the construction budget to create any sort of acoustical boundary between rooms. So their fight was our fight.

And that's when Scoshi decided to join in. He jumped up from the pillow, crawled down through the center and up to the foot of the bed. And started with The Bark.

A writer such as myself has difficulty trying to communicate, with words, the sound of any bark, much less this particular one. "Woof" sounds too soft and fluffy. "Ruff, ruff, ruff" has some merit, but still sounds muffled and lacks the stridency. Scoshi's bark is a clear, open-throated attack with a short, delicate, staccato finish, the kind of sound you'd expect from belting out the word "r-r-rutt" in rapid fire. One bark barely ends before the next one begins. The sound practically consumes every calorie he has to burn, and once it starts, it will not stop.

I tried to quiet him. I shushed him. I held his snout shut. I even took him into the bathroom, hoping to distract him with the inspiring change of scenery. Nothing worked. He was having issues with the people next door, and he was willing to take it to a higher authority. He was quickly becoming the dog in the circle with the red line through it.

So it was no coincidence that the knock at the door was Woody Allen. It was the kind of double knock that sounded more like a warning shot across the bow, the kind that makes no apology for the interruption in it. It was also the kind of knock that seemed to trigger the apocalypse for Scoshi, and now he started barking like a machine gun at the motel room door. He threw his little body a full four feet from the edge of the bed against the door to let Woody know that this could get physical.

"Do you have a dog?" That was the greeting. The fact that the animal that I was holding back by the collar was trying to take him out at the ankles made any answer seem pointless.

"We don't accept dogs here," he said, reminding me that I, too, missed the announcement when we checked in.

"Did you see the signs at the office?" Again I was hammered with the obvious.

"I'm sorry, I was really tired, I'm sure I missed it," I mumbled meekly, trying to plead guilty to a lesser crime.

"I've already had a complaint. Stop by the office on the way out for a refund."

So that was it, the couple next door had turned us in. Thirty hours into the Epic Journey Across the Continent, we were being tossed out of the Cheapest Motel in America. As if to celebrate the sanctity of the moment, Scoshi was suddenly quiet.

I quickly gathered our belongings and repacked the trunk. Scoshi quickly hunted for a new spot in the car to rest. An envelope with a credit slip was waiting for me on the office counter. Woody Allen was on the phone and didn't even bother to look up. Chances are he was talking again to Ozzie and Harriet in the next room because before I shut the door to our room, I changed the television channel to the Shopping Channel and turned the volume all the way up. It was my way of lifting my leg and leaving my mark.

We headed back into the night, and a short time later found a place to stay that welcomed dogs and their disgraced owners alike.

After that, the trip was less about adventure than it was about reflection. I continued to let Scoshi drive on my lap to pass the time and amuse the passersby. But my brain was busy hosting a party of thoughts, some important and some ridiculously trivial. But the most curious of all was The Bark.

I couldn't fault Scoshi for barking. He was now buried deep among the boxes in the backseat, and well past the point of caring. I had also licked my wounds and had pretty much healed from the embarrassment of the prior night's incident.

But there was something admirable in that bark that made it worth considering.

A dog's bark is as much a signature as its scent. Every bark is a full, clear statement of existence — "I bark, therefore I am." It is unrestrained, unedited, and unabashed. It has individual character and specific meaning. And all these qualities, strangely enough, are the same elements that, too often, separate the bark from the human voice.

I was standing at an airline ticket counter recently, completing the normal process of checking in. A woman standing at the counter next to me was having a difficult time trying to flag down anyone to answer a quick question. Person after person passed by her behind the counter while she timidly mouthed "excuse me" to each. More passed by. No one seemed to notice her, nor did she command anyone's attention. Except mine. I realized her plight and asked my ticket agent to pause long enough to answer her question. The woman thanked me in the same little voice and walked away.

How sad, I thought, to go through life without a bark. To live without a way to make a sound significant enough that says my concerns have merit. I thought of Scoshi in the motel room wailing a warning. I thought of every dog that has ever howled at the moon. No dog barks without total commitment to the sound and the meaning of that verbal gesture.

Short of having physical defects, most of us shrink our own voices. As infants we all barked. We expressed it by crying. Watch a child cry and you will see the proper use of the human voice. Focused perfectly in the facial mask and fully supported by the abdominal muscles, an infant crying is the perfection of expression. Soon, however, we are told not to cry. When we learn to speak, we are told to speak quietly. We grow up editing the sound of our voices. Dogs don't know how to do this. They grow up with a bark, and it has a simple on and off switch.

Over time, some of us develop lazy habits that obstruct our voices. We place the voice so far back in our throats that we strain our vocal cords hoarse at something as exciting as a college football game. Some lose their voices after a particularly ambitious stab at karaoke (which I've always maintained is the perfect activity for people who shouldn't drink and people who shouldn't sing).

A dog never strains or loses its voice. There's a black Labrador retriever down the block from us now in L.A. that confirms this premise every morning at sunrise. For thirty minutes every day we listen to a bark that is properly placed and properly supported and commands attention. And if I could throw a slipper a half a block I'd try to congratulate him on making that point.

Dogs instinctively speak correctly. Imagine how much more successful we could be if we used our barks. Imagine how much impact we could make by simply speaking with full, natural resonance instead of shrouding the sound with poor placement and sloppy enunciation. Imagine if we thought of our voices as genuine instruments of communication rather than as vehicles of apology.

Many of us have learned to dislike the sound of our voices, perhaps because we heard a recording of it from a friend's wedding reception video or on an answering machine. But the truth is, no microphone ever designed, least of all the cheap ones, can pick up the full ambient range of the human voice. They pick up a flat, one-dimensional sound. Motion picture studios spend much of their production budgets on sound experts who try to re-create the sound that you hear naturally when someone speaks. A dog never thinks about the sound of its bark; dogs are too busy trying to do something with it.

Strangely enough, we all speak correctly at certain times and aren't aware of it. When you hail a cab from across the street you are speaking correctly. Try "Hey, taxi!" using the same swallowed half-voice that you use to say "l'oh?" when you answer the phone — you'll be standing on that street corner a long, long time. Volume alone is not the issue here. Resonance and vocal support carry the voice a lot farther than volume does. Even the smallest dog can be heard from blocks away.

Dogs are also blessed with another virtue — silence. They only bark because they need to and for as long as they need to, as though they have an innate sense of self-editing. A dog never has to take back what's been said. A dog will never bark and lie. A bark always tells the truth.

Those were the lessons of that part of our journey. I'm sure there were others, but these are the ones that stayed with me. A bark says who we are and what we stand for. Perhaps if I'd used mine more prudently, my first marriage wouldn't have ended so abruptly. Perhaps this trip would not have been necessary at all. I'll never know.

Years have passed since then, and my partner on that journey lies at my feet now unable to hear. The years have taken that away from him, and now he barks, I guess, from habit. He's a bit wobblier as well. At this moment, I'm watching him try to scratch his ear with his hind leg without toppling over. But the same gentle stare is still there, as well as the slight tilt of the head to indicate that life is still a wonder for him. Our trip across the country was a trip across my life. I've eaten in life's strange places. I've stopped along the way in my life and have been unaccepted absolutely, occasionally with a circle and red line through it to further make the point. But to make the journey, to go through life and call it your own, you have to be heard. You have to have a bark.

IT'S OKAY TO MISS THE BED ON THE FIRST JUMP

It's not what happens to us in life, it's what we do about it that is the true measure of success. How we fail and how we recover says much about the character of our achievements. My life has been filled with constant reminders of the truth inherent in this premise. This life lesson was poignantly demonstrated recently by what some might consider the oddest of teachers — my dog Betty.

At first glance, Betty doesn't seem poised for this type of greatness. You don't have to watch her for very long to realize that she was put together with spare parts. Since she was a rescue dog I could never be certain of the bloodline, but most veterinarians seem pretty certain that she is a dachshund and black Labrador retriever mix. This blend has left her with the look of a perpetual puppy. Her coat is Elvis blue-black with brilliantine sheen and the occasional cropping of gray hair, which I don't suspect is as much a sign of her age as it is sympathy for mine.

Her little ears are never really sure of their place. In their starting position they are draped like little canopies. But with the slightest move of a muscle one will flip over inside out and stay that way until she shakes her head or my wife or I reach down and flip it back over. As Betty is listening to you she can make them dance up and down one at a time. I can do this with my eyebrows, which scares young children, but on Betty the little ear dance is another sign of endearment. On rare occasions she will twitch with enough force to turn both ears inside out, giving her a kind of upturned, Sandra Dee look.

Betty runs on three legs. She never runs on the same three, so I can't claim injury or ailment to be the source of her choice. She simply picks three, lifts one and darts off, like she always carries a spare tire. It's a fascinating display of energy conservation.

She has also earned the nickname "The Little Anvil," for the fact that she has curiously packed so much weight into her small, tubular frame without ever appearing overweight. Not until she steps on you in the morning to begin a custom that my wife affectionately terms the Love Fest do you realize that Betty is like a sausage that some generous butcher stuffed with an extra scoop. All that and an alligator tail that never stops moving.

Yes, the Love Fest begins each morning as the first crack of light dapples the bedroom through the plantation shutters. We could darken the room more, I suppose, but then we would all sleep until noon. Betty is definitely a morning dog.

The Love Fest is a fifteen-minute ritual with Betty, Scoshi, my wife, and me. It's a celebration of morning light and an upcoming meal with a lot of hugging and licking. The only rule seems to be: it can't stop. The dogs made up that rule. If you try to stop, Betty will submarine your hand back into position to pet. Scoshi will slap at you with his paw to remind you that it's still not enough. Then he starts sneezing. He has morning allergies, and he doesn't mind sharing them with you. As you pet one dog, the other will muscle in. This cluster of affection continues and, all the while, Scoshi is sneezing and Betty is smacking all of us with the alligator tail. Another day begins.

I guess our bed is pretty much the heart of the world in our house. In addition to being the site of the Love Fest, it is the center of all napping, the drop-off point for all Betty's plush toys, including Dinosaur, Santa Claus, and the Little Yellow Man, as well as the final resting point for all four of us each night as we jockey for a more comfortable position to sleep.

We didn't choose the bed with them in mind. It's a high canopy bed, fluffy and feather-downed, the kind you expect in a country inn. It's a gentle reminder to us to live like we're on vacation. Or at least sleep like it. The dogs decided between themselves that this is where they were going to sleep. Scoshi sleeps perched above my wife's head. He used to sleep over my head until my wife assumed feeding duty. Then he decided that she needed all the shrouding and protection he could give. Betty simply muscles a position in between us.

There is a bench at the base of the bed that serves as a launchpad for them to make the leap up. It also serves as the periodic depository of anything for which I'm too lazy to find an appropriate place — more easily defined as "stuff." This stuff never leaves. It just gets reshaped each week by our cleaning lady, who can't seem to think of an appropriate place for it either.

One night as the lights were going out at the heart of our world, Scoshi, our Maltese, was beginning to shroud my wife's head. I was trying to choose a position for my pillow that wouldn't cauliflower my ear, and from nowhere there was a sudden crash to the floor as though someone had dropped twenty pounds of sand. Betty had apparently tried to take the bed in a single leap instead of using the obstacle bench. I looked over the edge to see her on her side, scrambling to get back upright, both of her ears flipped over to underscore the concussion of the fall on the hard wooden floor. She got to all fours, shook her ears back into position, walked around to the foot of the bed, jumped up on the bench to the bed, and quietly snuggled in between us without any further ceremony.

As sudden and catastrophic as this was for her, I found it to be a very compelling moment. As I was petting her head to sleep that night, I was struck by the idea of missing the bed on the first jump and the deeper meaning in what was the simplest of misjudgments.

Betty leapt well beyond her abilities to a height twice her own, and yet, in her mind, she leapt for the most important of reasons. She knew the Love Fest didn't take place on the floor. If she was going to be part of it, she had to go to the source. Her subsequent face-plant on the floor didn't deter her from her deeper purpose. She simply shook herself off and found another route to her goal. Yes, she failed at first, but just long enough to give preparation a chance to catch up with opportunity.

The wonderful, reaffirming message of this incident is that just because we fail doesn't mean we are failures. It's okay to miss the bed on the first jump, and the second, and the third. It's okay to try another route. It is not okay to lose sight of the top of the bed and surrender our goal.

Achievement is one of the most important elements of the human experience. Along with acts of love and compassion, it is one of the fundamentals that give our lives meaning. A life devoid of achievement is a life wasted. It is as simple and brutal as that.

What is fascinating about dogs is they innately seem to get this. I've never known a dog that lived life as though it was just a rehearsal. Dogs focus on what they want and go for it. We people often live our lives like we are going to do it all over again, and the next time around we'll take all the chances. I am fascinated by the number of people I meet who continually disconnect from their goals and dreams, and I am continually frustrated with myself when I cast aside my own. Inasmuch as Betty's leap and free fall was a tough example of the act of achievement, it was just as much a gentle illustration of the elements of success.

Most important, Betty had a goal. She knew where she was and where she wanted to be. For many of us this is the hardest part. Where are we now? What are our goals? Self-assessment and goal-definition are often the biggest logjams to the flow of achievement. Many of us are unhappy in our present state and are not fully aware of it. We mask our disenchantment with drugs, alcohol, or other destructive behavior so we are physically and mentally unable to be accountable for it. Sometimes we intentionally become victims of our circumstances in life in an unconscious effort to avoid taking responsibility for a positive self-appraisal. How many times have you heard someone say, "I really wanted to do____, but I couldn't because____." You can fill in the blanks with your own answers because we have all spoken those words. My reply to that now is simply, "What would Betty do?"

I sifted through this cloud of delusion for a short time after college. It was one of the most uncomfortable periods of my life. Since I was three years old — old enough to point at the television — I knew I wanted to be an actor. I would display a certain amount of precocious disgust when anyone asked me what I wanted to be when I grew up. I would simply point back to the television, put my hands on my hips, and say, "Well, I am an actor, so that's what I'm gonna be." I would perform in talent shows, do skits in grade school, audition for every play in high school, and finally majored in theater and voice in college — all with pinpoint definition of where I wanted my life to go. That was, until a month before graduation. All of my friends were lining up their future plans. Some were going to medical school, others to law school. Some were getting actual jobs in sales or accounting with prestigious firms. I was going to be an actor, and for the first time in my life I had no idea how I was going to make a living at it.

I won the Theater Award at graduation, which was a source of enormous pride for me. I had to balance the glory of that achievement with perspective that there was no one else to give it to — I was the only graduating theater major. There was no directory of theater alumni to call on for help. I had no theatrical agent. In fact, I had only been to New York City twice in my life. At the most important crossroads of my young life, I was paralyzed by the business of show business. I let my circumstances dictate my purpose.

So I settled for less, and I got less. Shortly after graduation I got a job wrapping boxes in an advertising agency. Over the next five years I mildly fought my way through several positions in marketing and public relations. I also had developed insomnia. I couldn't sleep peacefully through the night. I had recurring dreams of being in fistfights with my arms frozen in slow motion. Or being unable to run from whatever was chasing me. I was simply playing out the frustration of following the wrong path in my life. The dark of night holds inescapable moments of honesty.

The sleeplessness and bad dreams stopped some five years later when I resigned from my post in public relations, sold off all but my most essential possessions, and went to live an actor's life in New York City. Twenty-five years have passed since I made that decision. There have been times since then when I thought I was the worst actor in the world, but it's been twenty-five years without regret.

Dogs, however, have no delusions about self-assessment. They are always pretty clear with how they feel about themselves. If they're satisfied where they are in life at any one moment, they'll wrestle a toy or take a nap to celebrate. When they find themselves in circumstances that are particularly unappealing, they'll do everything possible — bark, cry, scratch, or jump — to stack the deck back in their favor. As the lights went out in our bedroom that night, Betty knew, without complication, that she didn't want to be left on the floor. That is the clarity that we need to pursue a goal.

But how do we know what our goals are? We all have things we'd like to do. We have places we'd like to visit. We have changes in diet and behavior that we'd like to effect. We have careers we'd like to pursue. But are they our goals, or just a series of pleasant visuals that periodically pass through our minds? At what point do our imaginations stop entertaining us and actually instruct us?

The answer lies in our daydreams. That's right, daydreams. The thing the teacher told us not to do in school. Our daydreams don't lie to us. Daydreams are the part of the imagination where our inner self, with all our wishes and wants, surfaces long enough to reveal where we should be going in our lives. It's like a little movie theater that only plays previews of coming attractions, and we're the star of every feature. The more persistent the daydream the more meaningful the message. What we daydream about is what we should be doing.

When we come to terms with what we should be doing, we do what Betty did — we leap toward it. We leap because where we are is not where we want to be. We leap because any goal worth daydreaming about is not a step away; it is a leap away. It is the distance-leap that provides both the challenge and the satisfaction.

Finally, when we leap, we must leap as though the net will appear. A leap in life, however big or small, is an act of commitment with the expectation of success. The strength to leap comes from an unshakable sense of purpose. But we cannot leap expecting to get halfway there. If we miss the bed on the first jump, we try again, or we try another route. We do not surrender our goal.

Perhaps the message of "leaping" is what kept me "dancing" during my appearance as a celebrity ballroom dancer in the ABC competitive reality television show *Dancing with the Stars*. The show had everything that made it compelling entertainment — beautiful dancing, elegant costumes, dramatic lighting, wonderful music, and live competition. I was never working from the point of my strength; I wasn't acting; I wasn't singing. I was ballroom dancing — something I had never done before in my life, and now I was doing it in front of the entire country.

I took on the challenge of the competition much like Betty's jump. I knew where I was, where I wanted to go, and why I wanted to get there. And every week, when the orchestra conductor's baton dropped and the music wailed, a live television audience of 25 million people would watch me take one of the biggest leaps of my life across a hundred-foot stage, hoping a net would appear. It always did.

I wanted to win, not for the trophy and/or for the satisfaction of beating other people (because there really is none), but to reaffirm something that I have always believed — there is no value to a half-hearted effort; anything worth doing is worth doing as well as you can. For me, it was the meeting point of opportunity and preparation.

Betty sleeps quite comfortably right now, snuggling in between us like a chaperon, stealing as much warmth as she can for herself. The Love Fest is only eight hours away. I have often felt that a sleep this serene is earned, not given. It is the slumber of satisfaction and of balance. It is a sleep of accomplishment, one that I missed for several wayward years. But in the stillness of the moment, interrupted only by her gentle snores, Betty is a quiet and constant reminder to me: At least I jumped, how about you?

A COLD CAN OF MEAT IS STILL A FEAST

It was a simple experiment that proved, among other things, that I am capable of using my powers for good as well as for evil. Several years ago, I was hosting the popular syndicated game show *To Tell the Truth.* It was one of those classic game shows that pitted a person of notoriety, along with two imposters, against a celebrity panel who would, through the shrewdness of their questioning, try to figure out who the person of interest was and who the imposters were. It spawned the cult-classic phrase, "Will the real so-and-so please stand up?"

My celebrity panel was constantly brilliant. It was composed of the quick wits Meshach Taylor, Paula Poundstone, Brad Sherwood, Dave Coulier, and Brooke Burns, among others. I was amazed by their ability to comically divine information from our guests, as well as their ability to constantly entertain me as host. The producers and I felt an obligation to find interesting little ways to amuse them as well.

During one particular game, I had a plate of food placed in front of each member of the celebrity panel. The food was a typical stew — meat, potatoes, and vegetables in brown gravy, served warm. I asked them to sample the stew before I read aloud the sworn affidavit of our person of interest. And while they were happily munching away bite after bite, I informed them that what they were dining on so enjoyably was dog food — the first ever approved by the Food and Drug Administration for human consumption. One of them made a simply disgusted face, two spit the food out all over the desk, and the last left the stage physically ill.

Perhaps there is something suspect in my character that I still find this story amusing, not as much for the visual memory of watching them, on precious network time, turn the stage into a spittoon, but because it calls to mind the curious point that what is a delicacy to some, to others is not.

Scoshi, my white Maltese, has, for his entire life, been testing the boundaries of what is edible and what is not. As a puppy, you could hold him fully in the cup of your hand, which meant each of your fingers was food. If you brought him up to your face to nuzzle him or give him a kiss, it brought your nose, lips, and ears into play. If you laid him on your chest, he would try to tear loose a mouthful of sweatshirt. In any posture or position, he was clearly the consummate consumer.

As a puppy, Scoshi was particularly obsessed with luggage, not as much with the outbound suitcase as the inbound baggage. Returning luggage contained all sorts of possibilities — hotel cookies, airline chips, all mixed up with my scent on my clothes. So he would unpack for me. He'd methodically drag everything out of the suitcase and onto the floor with his teeth, sort out the edible from the possibly edible and eat what he could. Then he would take out all my clothes, spread them all over the house, and roll all over them with the intention of replacing the foreign smells with his own bouquet. Once, while living in an apartment complex in Hollywood with a common outdoor courtyard, I returned one day to find I'd left my door open. All of my clothes were strewn about the courtyard, and Scoshi was lying, belly-up, on a pair of my underwear — briefs, not boxers.

Food rules his life. Outside of napping, which he does at Olympic caliber, food is the focus of his existence. It is the only reason he bothered to learn how to sit, shake, dance, lie down, and roll over. Food would follow. It is the reason, I suspect, that he follows my wife, Lisa, step by step, room to room, all around the house every moment of the day. Since our marriage in 2004, she has assumed the title of the Great Feeder, and any move she makes could be toward the kitchen, which for our dogs is the Center of All Great Things That Could Possibly Happen.

It should come as no surprise, then, that directly following the Love Fest, each day at our house begins with the Great Event, triggered with such formulaic accuracy that we have long since given up the notion of using an alarm to wake us. Betty, our rescued dachshund/black Lab mix, takes care of that. She is in charge of the Beginning of Time every morning, a duty she discharges with nuclear precision. She has taken over the role of timekeeper as Scoshi has grown older and deafer and would sleep till noon with the luxury of a retiree if he could. But were he more compos mentis, he would regale you for hours with stories of the years he rose at dawn to lead the morning charge to breakfast.

But now it is in a woman's hands, and in

a kinder, gentler way, Betty begins the Great Event each morning with her own special fairy-tale touch — a kiss. Since our marriage, everyone has repositioned toward my wife's side of the bed — including me. Scoshi shrouds my wife's head on her pillow like a furry little white halo. Betty, who would shiver in a furnace, has used the night to burrow deeper and deeper under the blanket. Anytime any of us moves, we all jockey for a new position around my wife. By daybreak we resemble a Love Pretzel.

From this position, and at a time known only to her, but never later nor earlier than 6:30 a.m. on the atomic clock, Betty will stir from the womb of the bed. She will crawl quietly, considerately, and deliberately to surface for air. I feel her coming toward the top of the covers, as does my wife, but we let the events unfold as they will. Never disturb the Beginning of Time.

She emerges to new light as politely as she lives her life, with a kind of half-apologetic grace, not toward me, but toward the Great Feeder. She narrows her little black snout to within an inch of my wife's face and then it happens. Her little pink tongue comes out; she leans in a little more and gently kisses my wife's cheek.

What makes this kiss so important, so

meaningful, is not as much its purpose as its uniqueness. It is the only kiss that Betty will give all day. That's it. Yes, you can try for a midday smooch or a kiss goodnight, but it's not going to happen. Betty will only kiss once at dawn. And my wife is the object of her affection.

For the simple fear of truth, I have never asked my wife which of us kisses better.

The kiss stirs our hearts and stirs us from sleep. And it's usually enough commotion to stir Scoshi as well. His head will pop up, and his little button black eyes give us a bewildered look, not quite sure where he is or who we are. His hair is matted against the side of his face from the way he slept. But with a shake of the head, he reshapes himself, and returns to the land of the living.

The Ol' Love Fest takes place before the parade begins. When all the hugging, the rubbing, and the licking subsides, and my wife and I make the first move to the floor, you'd think it was a Hallmark Christmas morning or a bridal sale at Filene's. Betty hits the floor first, and usually with such a thud that you'd think it might not hurt her to skip a meal or two. She follows with a kind of panting whimper, which is her way to signal a profound event is about to happen. We're next, followed by Scoshi, whose aging little joints cause him to limp to the edge of the bed. My wife, with the instinct that made God grant motherhood only to women, picks him up and sets him gently on the floor. Then he tries to catch up to Betty with the run of a little old man, quietly panting, "I'm comin', I'm comin'."

Betty has already been down three flights of stairs, out to the kitchen, and back before we are even down the first flight. She'll run this path three or four more times, still panting and whimpering, in an attempt to guide us in case we forgot where the kitchen is.

The door swings open; they enter first, like bulls running the streets of Pamplona. There is barking, there is panting, there is whimpering. In a single, electric moment that wipes away the residue of any half-sleep, you know that you have arrived at the kitchen. In that one moment you appreciate why this is truly the Center of All Great Things That Could Possibly Happen.

For many years until recently, I was the Great Feeder. It was not a title I necessarily deserved, but one that was thrust upon me. Before my present wife, I was the only one of the three of us with opposable thumbs and a working knowledge of the can opener. For all those years, I would open the same can of meat at the same time each morning, split the can in the same equal portions, mash it up, let them both lick the spoon, and then set the porcelain double bowl down before them. A bowl of crunchies came later on in the day at Happy Hour.

All of that has changed, for the better, I'm sure. My wife instituted a regime change quietly one day, a kind of silent coup d'état. I couldn't give you a date or a reason. All I remember is that one day the chipped porcelain bowl was gone. The cases of cans of meat all with the same name were gone. The forty-pound sack of croutonlike dry crunchies, which I only had to refresh once a year, was gone, too. In their place — a stainless steel oversized double bowl with a smart, red enamel trim. A matching water bowl. Cases of the FDA-approved canned meat with garden vegetables, suitable for both pets and celebrity game-show panels. And a smaller sack of moist crunchies, with both a meaty, palatable scent and an expiration date.

And gravy. Yes, gravy. Bottles of three different flavors of canine gravy.

This was not just a discretionary shift in diet; this was a quantum leap from Stone Age to Renaissance.

The dogs not only no longer consider me

the Great Feeder, but any movement I make toward the kitchen is now met with double disinterest. I'm all right with this, I really am. It's an emotional demotion for sure, but a necessary one. I find solace in the fact that I'm simply a product of my long, personal relationship with food.

If I liked something, as a youngster, I ate it. In fact, I ate a lot of it. And I ate it often. Milk, I liked. I'd consume about thirty glasses at every meal, maybe a hundred. I'd down every bite of food with milk; I'd dunk my dessert in it. It was probably my primary source of protein through puberty. All I know is the day I discovered beer and wine, the bottom fell out of the agricultural commodities market.

I also liked tomato soup, which, coincidentally, I would make with milk. I liked tomato soup so much, in fact, that a college girlfriend actually bought me seventy-two cans of Campbell's Tomato Soup as a Christmas present one year. To date, it is one of the most thoughtful gifts I have ever received, and it only lasted about half of that winter.

So it's no surprise that I introduced the same unconscious monotony to the care and feeding of my dogs. What is a surprise to me is that they still responded with the same reckless joie de vivre that they now have for the culinary cabaret my wife prepares for them each morning; except for the kiss — that's new, and something between them. But I got the same parade to the kitchen, the same panting, whining, and barking. I got the same unspeakable swirl of excitement and anticipation as a new day and a new meal lay in wait. Nothing changed, only the menu and the management.

What is instantly apparent in all of this is a simple truth — to a dog, a cold can of meat is still a feast. Their instinct is to recognize the simple grace in substance over style, the value of function over form. This is not so much the lesson of toleration as the lesson of appreciation.

They recognize that we provide for them what they cannot provide for themselves. They love us for the kindness of that responsibility. We love them for the joy and affection that they return. It is a perfect, constantly renewing circle. A circle, in our house, interrupted only by the occasional puddle of pee.

Appreciation is a lost art — at least in me. I find myself caught continually in the sad paradox that as I age I have to fight to appreciate more, without realizing that as I age I simply have more to appreciate. I send fewer thank-you notes, return fewer calls. I distract myself with distraction often to avoid the joy of a spontaneous moment or a conversation with a stranger in an elevator.

Appreciation, it seems to me, has an all-consuming, natural enemy. It is the arrogance of presumption. The more I have, the more I assume, and the less I appreciate. There is a universal tension between assumption and appreciation, and it never gives up.

My first car cost most of my personal fortune at age nineteen — one hundred dollars. And it was worth every penny of that. It was a twenty-year-old, paint-faded, bluish convertible with a leaky roof and a leaky transmission, which seemed to favor neutral and reverse over the stress of any other direction. Yet for that one moment in time it was the treasure of personal freedom, a magic carpet that I could hitch to my every whim. I would glance out the window at night to admire it. I would run down the stairs in the morning to make sure it was still there.

Today, the style of a car has replaced its function. The convenience of a car has replaced the wonder of its purpose. I move in and out of a car lease with the predictability of a thirty-six-month locust. I no longer appreciate the presence of an automobile; I take for granted its inevitability.

Yet our two dogs begin each day with nothing. The trip down to the kitchen seems to come each day as an unexpected surprise to them, as it did to me to find my car still in the driveway. They end the day with nothing more than the bond of our companionship and the comfort that, together, we continue to survive another day.

Now, I'm not suggesting that we can appreciate everything. None of us has the time, the capacity, or the awareness to give the universe its full due. We have a right to a certain amount of self-involvement. It's as human as it is important. It's what makes us interesting. I had two great-aunts who seemed to appreciate everything, and as sweet as they were, I couldn't spend a lot of time around them. They seemed to have neglected their own self-interests in favor of appreciating everyone else's. They were simply too easy an audience.

I also think it's safe to assume some things without appreciating them. Like gravity. I personally don't spend any time appreciating gravity, and I'm comfortable with that. I acknowledge it, I respect it, but I also expect it to be there each day. The instant it isn't, I'll simply shoot around the room backward for thirty seconds and then cease to exist.

Now, if I were a cosmetic surgeon in Beverly Hills I would feel differently. I would hope gravity would draw me to my knees each day. I would express in prayer my appreciation for the effects of the gravitational pull that seemed to fill my office with patients each day.

For my dogs there is always time to appreciate the simple joys of life — the pomp and parade to the kitchen each morning, riding with their heads out the window, or chasing the Wicked Witch, the toy of the moment, down the hall until she bounces off enough furniture to come to a rest on the floor, when she will then get the shaking of her life. There's the soft feel of the grass in the backyard, always worthy of a roll or two. There's the singular sound of the word "walk," which apparently sounds like "lotto winner" to them. And, of course, there's the unexpected joy of a suitcase that returns home. The list is endless, and the list is repetitive. And they are always as grateful as if it were the first time.

As my wife has taught me to love more deeply, my dogs have taught me to appreciate more fully and assume much less. Appreciation, for me, is an act of humility, a way to acknowledge what we cannot or did not do for ourselves. It sets a balance between being individual acts of self-fulfillment and being simple creatures of need.

The fact that I can have a dog as a pet and companion means that my life is filled with abundance. If I can recognize that, then every day is the Beginning of Time, and the whole world is the Center of All Great Things That Could Possibly Happen.

EVERY FIFTEEN
MINUTES IS A
BRAND-NEW DAY

I'm not sure when my obsession with the mail delivery began. It wouldn't surprise me if shortly after the cutting of my umbilical cord I crawled instinctively in the direction of the mailbox, like a baby turtle finding its way to Mother Sea. I realized early on, for one moment a day, that big aluminum tube at the end of the driveway was a connection to the world.

It was at a time before e-mails and the third-class deluge, back when the mail contained actual letters written in skilled penmanship by the human hand; back when letters were an exchange of ideas and events, of love and hope, of regret and sorrow. All of that, plus, if it was a birthday or Christmas card from my two aunts, it also contained twenty bucks.

Today my penmanship is miserable. If I had to write my own ransom note, my life would be over. The few hen scratches I make now are on checks, and only because the world of online banking still baffles me. I type my ideas, as I'm doing now. I e-mail in memo form instead of scribing any thoughtful correspondence. Instead of licking a stamp, now I press "Enter."

My keenness for the mail, however, has not dimmed a bit. Today it is for different reasons. The mail still contains a few items of interest, magazines, invitations, and the occasional card or note. But mostly it is a pile of catalogs, the result of purchasing a turtleneck by mail order seven years ago. The smoke signal from that stunning mercantile event spread far enough that not only does every clothing company now hope I will repeat the experience with them, but others trust that it also will inspire me to refinance my home, travel to the Caribbean, and steam-clean my carpets. Come Christmas, the density of silly mail reaches critical mass, and I need a team of Sherpas to make the daily postal trek.

But regardless of this, today I make the trip to the mailbox because it always makes me laugh.

Anytime my wife or I leave the house through the front door, Betty and Scoshi gather together for the long goodbye. They sit in silence by the door with orphan eyes in a last-ditch attempt to talk us out of leaving without them, or leaving at all.

When I go for the mail I get the same sad ceremony. I look back up the stairway to the door and there are four little cookie eyes and two cheerless little faces pressed against the glass, neither believing nor understanding why I would break up the family like this, and wondering if I'll ever return.

I'm gone to the end of the driveway and back in possibly two minutes. I return to a hero's welcome.

Betty is leaping and yelping. Scoshi barks and turns circles. They won't stop until I put the mail down and hold each of their faces in my hands so they can look me in the eye and see for themselves that *it is really me.* I'm home again and the family is intact once more.

That is now why I love to get the mail. It reminds me that dogs live, more or less, without the burden of time.

I actually believe that dogs live in fifteen-minute increments, that every fifteen minutes is a brand-new day. If you don't believe me, try and reprimand a dog for a puddle she left twenty minutes ago. She will look guilt-free. Time has already absolved her of responsibility. If you do catch the dog within the fifteen minutes, he will forgive himself long before you will.

It's not that dogs can't remember. You can condition their behavior; teach them to sit, lie down, fetch a Frisbee. It's that dogs just don't need to remember much. They don't have expectations beyond their immediate needs. They're not obsessed with their potential. They're not crippled by regret.

Dogs live totally in the present moment. When you are there, they are happy. When you close the door behind you to leave, they think you are still standing there on the other side of it, and they're not happy. Their relationship with time is a good deal different from ours. In many ways, it's a good deal healthier.

Time is the measure of all human activity. We cannot even conceive of something free of time. It is the means by which we track every occurrence. Our languages are structured to explain how we manage time. Verbs have tenses — past, present, and future. Music has tempo. Sports have stopwatches, shooting clocks, speedometers, and penalties for delay of the game. We even call "time-outs," which may temporarily placate the coach, the team, and the fans, but in truth is a fallacy. Time never really stopped. And that is the harsh reality.

It's not our obsession with time that

causes complications in our lives. It's that we can't escape it. It is the one omnipresent trademark of the human experience. From the moment we are born our sliver of time begins ticking like a taxi meter. None of us knows for how long.

How do we manage the profound reality that time, especially our piece of it, is finite? Our answers directly depict the quality of our lives.

I remember being fascinated by time as a youngster. Not telling time, which I learned at the same age that everyone else did, but contemplating the idea of infinity, that something like God had no beginning or end. I could spend hours trying to absorb the concept of "always was, always will be." This was scary stuff for me, a bit like standing on the edge of the garage roof and each time leaning a little farther out to see how far you could go without falling. I stopped imagining infinity when I felt my head overheating and my brain about to explode.

Later on, in college, I read a lot of T. S. Eliot, who peppered his epic poem *Four Quartets* with long reflections on Time Past, Time Present, and Time Future. Now, instead of mulling over the concepts of infinity and eternity, I would step to the far edge of the roof and ponder the impossible notion of Time Present. It seemed impossible because every present moment was past by the time you considered it. How can I live in the present moment if there is no such thing, if it was constantly whizzing past me faster than I could live in it? This was my first awareness of the problem of time.

(By the way, I blame Adam and Eve for the confusion. They bit into the Apple, committed the Original Sin, and were evicted from the Garden of Eden. Given some of the more poignant moments of my misspent youth, I argue that the penalty seems to me a bit severe. However, I actually don't think their punishment was relocation at all. As a consequence of the Original Indiscretion, which according to the Bible we have all inherited, I think God slapped them with the awareness and the burden of time. After all, if you're going to punish a woman, tell her she's going to age. If you're going to punish a man, tell him he doesn't have all of eternity to accomplish something. And, by the way, they're both naked.)

Since then, I have come to realize that time is a healer, when we allow it to heal us. It is a source of stress when we seem to have too little of it. It's the source of boredom if we have too much, and a cause of insanity in prison, where there is time and nothing else.

Time is chronological when we tag fossils and wine, when we pick planes and trains, when we make appointments and reservations. When time is spent in the arms of a lover or in the office of the school principal it is subjective and bears no relation to its temporal duration.

Time past is history, both in the epic and the personal sense. It is a great teacher of lessons learned and a great celebrator of monumental lives. Time future is our prophecies, dreams, and expectations.

It isn't the deepest of secrets that our lives are happiest when we live in the present moment, in Time Present. When we dwell on the past or put too much importance on the future it seems to put an unnatural drag on time, and it is the cause of stress and anxiety. The deeper secret is, how do we live in the present?

For as much as he confused me in my college days, T. S. Eliot did say something in *Four Quartets* that stayed with me — "be still, and wait without hope / For hope would be hope for the wrong thing." That was his explanation of how to live in the present moment.

That may seem like explaining the meaning of life with the lyrics to "The Hokey Pokey." It's expressive, but a little obtuse.

Fortunately, Betty and Scoshi provide a more practical application.

As I write this, I'm in New York working on Broadway, which has been as exciting for the dogs as it has been for my wife and me. I get to appear on Broadway six nights a week. They get to pee on Broadway four times a day. If your life consists of a constant search for appealing smells, you can't beat the streets of New York City. The first four inches from the ground up make this possibly the most exciting place on Earth.

Several nights ago, my wife was ill and sleeping deeply by the time I returned from the theater. It was my marital duty to perform the late-night walk. They were both sleeping quietly around my wife, helping her heal as best they could. I leaned over Betty, lifted her little black ear and whispered, "Wanna go for a walk?" She snapped up and shot out of the room like a bungee cord. Scoshi was sleeping in a halo around my wife's head and was a bit harder to extricate. His deafness and my inability to come up with a meaningful sign for "walk" made any attempt at communication pointless, but he eventually drafted off Betty's excitement as to why we were suddenly disturbing a pretty decent nap in the middle of the night. I picked him up gently to put him on the floor, and he picked up a clipped little stride as he headed out toward the door.

Betty was doing circles in the living room. She got the first leash; I think she regards this as a reward for being the most enthusiastic about the walk. Then I turned to Scoshi and put on his little red dog jacket, something my wife bought him to cut the winter chill. He resembled a kid wearing an ill-fitting Superman costume for Halloween.

I had just finished snapping Scoshi's buttons in place when I noticed the oddest thing. Betty was standing an inch from the door, leash lying at her side, staring at the tiny crack between the door and the jamb. Just staring.

I paused with Scoshi in my arms and waited. Betty continued staring, absolutely motionless. So I let her continue to stand and stare.

I slowly opened the door several minutes later. She tore down the hallway with her leash slapping behind her. I put Scoshi down, and we followed in pursuit down the hall to the elevator, where Betty was sitting and waiting.

I thought about Betty's strange posturing

as we took our meandering walk up Broadway at midnight. Her adrenaline rush off the bed and around the living room was so quickly replaced by an almost impenetrable stillness at the door. It was as though I had caught her in a private moment of contemplation, without expectation of when or even if the walk would ever begin. *Be still, and wait without hope / For hope would be hope for the wrong thing.*

We finished the walk after they'd fully doused Broadway. We got back to the apartment, I unsnapped their outfits, unleashed them, and we all got ready for bed. Betty crawled under the covers to burrow between us for the night. Oddly, though, Scoshi didn't return to his spot on my wife's pillow. He stood his ground on the edge of my pillow as I slid into bed. He was staring at me. Then he gave me his little tilt of the head, and continued staring.

So I stared back. At first, I was into the contest — who blinks first. His black marble eyes pierced through me in the dim light of the bedside lamp. For some reason he seemed locked on to me and wouldn't let go. The longer I stared, though, the more something changed inside me. It was like a quiet melting away of everything else that seemed to matter at the moment, including the contest. I just looked at him, and in his eyes I felt everything he felt, mostly his love. I felt the weight of our history together — our trip across the country, the many friends that have come and gone, and the many places we've called home. I was staring into the eyes of the puppy that had somehow and too suddenly become a little old man. In the same instant I felt the deepest joy for all of our years together mixed with a sad awareness that someday not too far off, those little eyes will be just a memory. I had brushed up against Time Present, and I read a million meanings into that one moment.

It actually lasted more than a moment. It was many, and Scoshi broke the stare first. He leaned into me, and there in the half light and the quiet of the night, he gently licked my face. The tears welled in my eyes. I looked over at my wife, who was sleeping deeply through her cold medication and sounding like her sinuses were barely open. I crawled across the bed and kissed her gently on the cheek. I was just sharing the love.

I fell asleep that night recalling another verse of Eliot's poem, "Time past and time future / What might have been and what has been / Point to one end, which is always present." It seems that love can only truly exist in the present moment, and only when we are present in that moment can we truly love.

T. S. Eliot and a couple of dogs made sense of that for me.

WHEN SOMEONE STOPS PETTING YOU, MOVE ON

I have a business partner, John, who is as shrewd as he is eloquent and funny. He has a dog, Reagan, who is as gracious as she is inspiring and enterprising. The shrewdness I have come to expect from John, as I've sometimes watched our fiscal honeydews turn to lemons, but then watched him squeeze lemonade from the rotting fruit. His sense of humor has made the financial recoveries much more palatable.

But Reagan is a constant wonder. She is an eighteen-year-old, honey-colored Labrador retriever with a smooth coat and soft, dark eyes. She has reached an age few dogs do and still does things each day most dogs never attempt. She swims morning laps in the pool, whether you'd like her to or not. She goes face-to-face daily with coyotes and the neighbor's caged mountain lions (odd neighborhood, I'll admit). Early each morning she'll bound down the long, curved driveway to bring back John's *Los Angeles Times.* If she can't find it, she'll bring back someone else's. If she beats the newspaper delivery, she'll bring back something that she thinks looks like a newspaper — a golf towel, a paper bag, even a branch. The trip down the driveway is never wasted.

Her enterprising nature was cultivated early in her puppy years. She was welcome in every home in the neighborhood, and she expressed her appreciation for that by picking up mementos from each house she visited. One neighbor lost a set of vice grips, another a cassette tape of the Guess Who. She even brought back a stainless steel and gold Rolex watch one day without much ceremony. She was on a constant salvage mission. The pattern and the value of her pickings made sense only to her.

One afternoon John was greeted by the sound of metal scraping up the driveway. The sound was getting louder and clearer. He opened the door to find Reagan dragging a nine-foot aluminum pool skimmer into the garage. Origin unknown. She had the netted end in her mouth while the long extension pole bounced along the pavement behind her. Apparently this was something no home should be without — or at least not John's. She dropped the little treasure off in the garage with the noticeable sense of fulfillment that she had made their home a bit more complete.

For all of her enthusiasm and her admirable commitment to retrieving, she had not exacted any sort of solid return policy. That was left to John, which I guess is one of the ways in which he developed his eloquence and sense of humor.

Reagan even helped John start his first business. At the bottom of his street in Houston, Texas, was what was called a "chug hole," a deep pothole that lay in wait to catch an unsuspecting driver. This was back when cars were more apt to have hubcaps than chrome rims. When a car hit the hole, the hubcap would fly off the wheel, then spin and dance down the street. This would signal Reagan to give chase. A rolling hubcap had an element of sport to it. She would bring them back to the garage, which soon began to look like the set of *Sanford and Son.* When the inventory was sufficient, John would ride his bike down to the local grocery store parking lot, scan the cars for missing hubcaps, and then sell them back to their owners for ten dollars apiece. They were a perfect team.

But there is something else in Reagan's character that intrigues me.

At heart, Reagan is a Southern belle. She always acts with a quiet graciousness that suggests her proper Texas upbringing. Always the perfect hostess, she greets all guests at the door, walks them into the living room, and sits patiently until they are seated. Then, in a most unimposing way, she will walk up to each person, rest her chin on their knee, and allow each to pet her for as long as they like.

When the petting stops, she politely moves on to the next. She makes no plea for continuity. She accepts that petting has a beginning and an end, and she knows that another pair of hands is waiting. She has performed this ritual for the many years I have known her.

Now, you can argue that there is much to glean from the entrepreneurial side of her temperament. And truly some may admire the whimsy and freedom of Reagan's carpe diem/carpe Rolex approach to life.

But for those, like myself, who are relentlessly self-improving, I find more illumination in Reagan's ability to courteously command attention and affection. And even more important, I respect her ability to know when it's time to move on.

Betty shows a similar color. She accompanies Scoshi when we take him to the veterinarian. As Scoshi gets older these trips have sadly become more frequent. While he shivers with anxiety, Betty uses the vet's waiting area like a Sunday social, a grand meet-and-greet. She tours the room, jumps into each owner's lap, and enjoys a few moments of affection. When the petting subsides, she then pays her respects to the accompanying dog, cat, bird, hamster, or reptile. She'll make her rounds until everyone has had a chance to appreciate her.

Again, as much as I admire her skill to attract attention, I am more impressed by Reagan and Betty's ability to let go so easily and purposefully. It is not the attachment I applaud, but the detachment.

I was not born with this quality. I know I am not alone in this.

I've spent many years of my life unable to let go. Relationships, career disappointments, even personal mistakes.

And often at the expense of my dignity.

It was at the age of fourteen that I stumbled into my first relationship with a girl. I say "stumbled" because I can't really pinpoint the day the teasing, the stalking, and the name-calling turned into secret phone calls and private walks.

But I do remember Halloween night that year. It was cold enough to need a coat, which sort of neutralized the effect of any snappy costume. But no matter. A pair of jeans and my navy surplus peacoat were fine — 'cause I was trick-or-treatin' with a girl.

I have no memory of candy, or costumes, or mischief that night. I only remember an exact spot on the sidewalk at the corner of our block. I remember the chill of my breath as I inhaled suddenly. I remember how stunningly silent the night seemed for one special moment in time. The entire world stood still just long enough as I reached down and, for the first time, I held her hand.

And I didn't let go for three hours.

About eleven o'clock that night her father showed up on our doorstep, none too pleased that his daughter had not returned home. He would have been a lot less pleased if he had seen me with a death grip on his daughter's right hand making our seventieth lap of the neighborhood. We were different religions — I was Catholic, she was Jewish, so I knew that fueled his discontent. But I was touching skin for the first time, and I was going to make it last.

But, as is often the case in male/female relationships, I couldn't.

The weight of attraction had clearly slipped to my side. While she was probably intrigued, she was not smitten. I, however, was heavily smote.

We went on a series of unspectacular dates. I took her to see the movie *Ice Station Zebra,* a film with Ernest Borgnine and several other male actors all stuck on the North Pole for the entire two hours. It had all the romance of a public hanging and was possibly the stupidest idea for a movie date ever. So I got no hand-holding in return.

That summer she went off to camp in New York State and I went to a rented cottage at the beach in Connecticut with my family. We kept in touch with letters. Mine were painfully sculpted. Each word chosen carefully or erased; each letter closed with the real intent of the note, "I Miss You."

Her letters back sounded like an ad for the summer camp. No "I Miss You, Too." I got the list of sports activities minus the phrase of significance. But still I would beat a path to the mailbox each day to wait for another. And I would race to the box to mail my "I Miss You" in return.

As much as this was my first experience with romance, it was also my first experience with the power of denial.

By September the phone calls were fewer and more strained. I would actually jot down notes before I called her to keep some kind of dialogue going. Kind of a cheat sheet for witty and charming discourse. But one night, a week before my birthday in early October, I let both ends of the conversation gap just long enough for her to slip in, "I don't think you should call me anymore." I was sunk by the sting of the words.

It was the end of hand-holding forever.

It was not the end of my grip on the relationship, however.

In the weeks that followed, I still rode my bike past her house at strategic times of the day. I'd toss a nonchalant but desperate glance in the direction of her window and then continue on till the end of the block. Then I'd turn around and pedal back to see if I'd had any impact. None. None at all. I even wrote her a letter. Nothing. Nothing at all. So there it was, I'd turned myself into fourteen-year-old cannon fodder.

It got worse, but to understand how much worse, you have to know that at that age, I went to a boys' school in the area that held a strict policy of mandatory sports for all students. That meant that no matter how bad you were, there was a team sport for you.

My poison was football.

I had a body that was better suited for the debate team than the gridiron. I was tall and very skinny. I was also a terribly slow runner. Add the weight of the football equipment to me and you could time my sprints with a calendar.

So despite the mandatory policy of participation, no coach in his right mind was going to risk a close game to give me a few character-building moments on the football field. So I sat for most games. I sat on a bench far from the starting team accompanied by a few other misfits. Our first game of the year we sat on a freshly painted green bench that had not fully dried in the chilly fall temperatures. It left a series of green stripes across the backs of our uniforms that never came out. From that moment we were unfairly branded the Green Paint Brigade. It is one thing to be untalented, and quite another to be notorious for it.

Our homecoming game was our first since the Breakup with the Girlfriend. It was also my birthday. Parents and alumni filled the bleachers on a beautiful, crisp October day in New England. My parents didn't come — it was a bit futile. Even they knew I wasn't going to play.

The school sports administrator was always careful to choose for the homecoming game an opposing school that we could easily pummel. It made a better show for the alumni and ensured us of at least one victory for the season.

It didn't mean, however, that I would play. So I just sat there, kicking my helmet occasionally and sharing small talk with the rest of Green Paint Brigade, and mildly watching our starting team on the field absolutely eviscerate the other school. Happy birthday to me.

The game reached the point of pointlessness late in the fourth quarter, when we were winning by a score of, to my memory, 17,000 to nothing. With two minutes left I began to realize that the coach either wanted to preserve the overwhelming shutout without the threat of my abilities, or else thought the game could still go either way. So I turned my head to casually scan the stands to see if I recognized any faces.

And I did. She was there.

My head snapped back. My mind raced. I stopped breathing. Had she been there the whole game? No. Please, please, please, no. I didn't play. I can't have her see me in my most emasculating of moments. Think. Think.

And that's when I chose a play that in football is called the old razzle-dazzle.

I was sitting at the far end of the bench, next to the steel water bucket. Slowly I reached my right hand down and scooped up a ladleful of water that I dumped over my head. I did it again. And again. And again, until I was pretty much marinated.

Then I bent over and grabbed a handful of dirt, which I mixed with a bit of water from the pail, and made a neat little mud pie. Still bent over, I started spreading it all over my face, arms, and legs. I sat back against the bench and continued smearing the mud over the front of my uniform. Meanwhile, I'm now watching the game clock for the first time. I'm sprinting to the goal line.

By the time the final gun sounded and the teams headed back to the sidelines, I looked like a marine recruitment poster or at least like I'd been dragged by a tractor through a pigsty. I quickly joined the starting team in the victory swirl that was gathering around the coach. We all threw our helmets to cheer the dead and wounded from the other school. No one seemed to notice that I'd oddly turned a muddy shade of brown. They must have figured I'd slipped and fell on my way to the end of the bench.

But they no longer concerned me. I had my eye on one girl in the stands.

As the cheers subsided, the players gathered their helmets and their egos and began their slow gladiatorial strut back to the field house. And I joined them. I passed just close enough to the emptying stands to make sure I was seen by the Important One. I moved slowly and deliberately across the adjoining field, picking up the rhythm of my team- mates. It was the swagger of John Wayne at the Alamo ready to whoop the entire Mexi- can army. My helmet hung by my side and I was breathing heavily — from the last two hours I spent sitting on a bench.

If it seems that I was chumming for atten- tion, very specific attention, then I didn't have to wait long for the first strike. It came up slowly from behind me. It met my stride and matched my pace.

She tapped me on the shoulder pads. Before I could say something heroic like "Hi," she cut in first.

"How come you're breathing so hard? You didn't play."

I had no response. She had just tackled me with her tongue. Then I remembered the Alamo. John Wayne got the swagger kicked out of him, too.

She didn't mean to clothesline me, either. I'd run right into the outstretched arm.

I fired back with something unmemorable while I tried to crawl into my football helmet. Then she said she had come with a bunch of friends to see a bunch of friends, and she had to get back to that bunch of friends, "So, bye!"

Yes, happy birthday to me.

I still carried the torch for her an Olympian distance after that. Another year of my young life. She'd moved on, but I was still running in place.

Two years later, at sixteen, I finally fell in love again. It was more serious this time because this bonding went way past hand-holding; it involved kissing. Unfortunately, I met her six weeks before my family was moving from Connecticut to Florida. It was like Romeo and Juliet, both torrid and doomed. We kissed for six weeks. In fact, it was a single, long, deep, six-week kiss broken up only by the plane door closing as I took off to a distant and sadder shore.

True to form, I spent every moment of my senior year in high school pining for someone a thousand miles away. She, on the other hand, mourned our loss for a solid month. Then she met a friend of her brother's who she eventually married.

Those are two years of my life I will never get back. And I miss them not for the quantity of time, but for the quality of those precious, pivotal years when there could have been so many healthier things to experience. But in my need to create reality out of the unreal, I became a victim of my own desperation, refusing to accept the simple dignity and inevitability of loss.

Loss is both inevitable and total. Accepting it is the gift. As I have grown older and life has become more complicated, I watch many friends now take the guidance of therapy. More often than not, they are coping with some form or consequence of loss — job, love, or life. It seems, too, that many are paralyzed by the process of healing. They live in the exhausting spiral of analysis without ever experiencing the gentle release of synthesis.

But in Reagan and Betty I see the balance of connection and disconnection. Reagan's head moves from knee to knee and Betty from lap to lap with neither ceremony nor regret. It is the gentle dance of analysis and synthesis.

It seems that in our search for a life with meaning there is the paradox that sometimes we let things mean too much. Whether you are grasping something as fragile as the heart or as gripping as the treasure of an aluminum pool skimmer, sooner or later, you have to let go.

Own Your Own Fur

One phone call can change your life. That is the one reality of my life that is easily the most fascinating. Because I'm an actor and an entertainer, I have had many more jobs than most people will have during the course of their lives. I have also gotten many of these life-altering phone calls.

I'll always remember one that came early on a Monday morning in August five years ago. I was sitting at my desk at home in Los Angeles at the time.

"Hello?" I said, aware that I've been using this greeting my entire life and still can't figure out what it means.

"Woof. Woof," was the response.

That was the beginning of my conversation with an executive at NBC Sports, and the beginning of the National Dog Show on NBC Thanksgiving Day.

In the five years since I got the unusual call to serve as host of the show along with dog expert David Frei, it has become the most enjoyable yearly event in my oddly eclectic career. Every November, it's a chance for my wife and I to spend a day in Philadelphia with two thousand of the most beautifully bred dogs in the country.

I have never claimed to be a dog expert. Fortunately, I have the savvy database of my cohost, Mr. Frei, to fill in all the important content about each of the more than 150 breeds that are represented at the show.

The first year of the National Dog Show was in 2002. That's when I began to cut my eyeteeth on the rich history of kennel clubs and canine breeding. I also learned the show is as much about the people as it is about the dogs.

It also gave me a chance to say some of the stupidest things I have ever said on television.

The Old English sheepdog and his handler stepped up to have their turn before the judge, an elegant woman in a long gray gown with the air of a mother superior. If you are not familiar with the sheepdog breed, it's about two pounds of actual dog and seventy pounds of long, stringy hair that completely camouflages the animal, including the face and eyes. It looks like a large cotton swab. The judge promptly went about her work, busily picking up clumps of hair on the dog's back and running her hands through the thick coat.

Over at the broadcast booth, I was watching this exercise with David and began my duties as host by asking all the intelligent questions.

"David, can you describe what she's doing." *Great beginning.*

"She's putting her hands on the dog, John, to check the alignment of the shoulders and the hips and make sure they meet the AKC guidelines for the confirmation. She has to get her hands under all that hair because you can hide a really bad dog with a really good haircut."

I said, "You're telling me. I went to junior prom." *Whoops.*

Then the judge walked around to the front of the dog and began picking up the hair on the dog's face and pulling it apart.

"What's she doing now, David?" *I've hit my stride now; this question is riveting.*

"She's checking the bone structure of the head and pulling back the hair to see the eyes and gauge the attentiveness of the dog," he said, barely having to think.

I said, "Well, if she picks through all that hair and finds only one eye, she's got the wrong end of the dog."

Oh, how had the dog show world survived without the benefit of my insight?

Despite these indiscretions at the microphone, which I seem to find a way to repeat each year, I come and go from the show each time with the same important impression — dogs like being dogs.

The National Dog Show is a benched show, and one of the last remaining. As such, it means that dogs and owners must remain in the arena for the duration of the event. The holding areas are open to the public, and anyone, especially children, can walk through the aisles, see each of the variety of breeds up close, and chat with the owners, handlers, and breeders. They get to watch the bathing, primping, and grooming that gets the dogs show-ready.

My wife and I make this trip through the aisles the highlight of our stay. There may be several acres of dogs in the one arena. The thing that hits me over and over again is that not one of the dogs really cares about the show. The show is for the people — the kennel club, network, owners, breeders, handlers, vendors, valet parkers, and the public. The dogs are just happy to be dogs and would be just as content rolled up in their favorite blanket back at home.

More to the main point, dogs like being

the dogs that they are. There is no sense of competition among them — even though the competition among them is the very essence of the event. I watch each dog enter the ring with a stride that reveals months or years of careful coaching. They stand before the judge with the patience of a saint as their bodies are picked at and examined from every angle. But that is where their investment in the occasion ends. They are not aware of their strengths or their weaknesses in their physical makeup. They are oblivious to the importance of the decisions being made about them. There are unaware if they win or lose. More often than not the losers will lick the winner, and the winner will sniff them all as they pass. For all of them it is simply a chance for a warm bath, a new haircut, some great food, a nice run around the ring, and a chance to mingle with a few of their own. All in all, a pretty pleasant day.

You never feel the tension of envy when standard poodles go head to head in their breed competition. When the toy group (the little yippy ones) enters the group ring, the Yorkshire terrier doesn't want to be a Chihuahua. The dachshund doesn't want to be a black Lab, although I do suspect some type of deep-seated affinity there, since

Betty is a mix of both.

We care more than they do. Best in Show feeds a fire in us that is unimportant to them.

I do visit arenas where that fire burns out of control. A beauty pageant is a five-alarm case in point, and I've had my chance to host a bundle; every shape, size, and level of pageantry. Young kids, teens, Miss, and Mrs. — even dogs in evening wear. I've sung a runway walking tune for them all. I've asked endless contestants in-the-spotlight questions about world peace and family values.

What makes a beauty pageant different is that the contestants care about the results. They have a lot invested in the outcome — the gowns, the makeup, in some cases the talent lessons. Then there's the travel and in other cases the cost of the cosmetic surgeon.

While I have proven beyond a doubt my lack of expertise when it comes to dogs, I also don't claim to be an authority on human behavior because I've been a television host. I can make, however, the observation that I don't feel the sense of innocent joy waiting in the wings of a beauty pageant as I do wandering the backstage of the National Dog Show. I do feel, amid the anticipation of the crowning and the excitement of being on television, the presence of envy in these pageants, and a kind of human score-keeping that seems to contradict the celebration onstage. I've watched temper tantrums because one contestant was upstaging another or because one took up too much space in a dressing room mirror.

When the tears and the shouting subside, and after the contestants have marched past the judges enough for them to make the most subjective of decisions, someone is finally crowned the Best and Most Beautiful. She walks down the aisle and begins her year of photo ops.

Now, I don't mean to wax so cynical — after all, I am often the one hosting these shows. I cowboy-up in my tuxedo and smile from ear to made-up ear. Silence deems consent. It is also not my purpose to preach, but you can't go through an experience like that and not suspect that this is not man (or woman) at their best; that these moments only seem to underscore a festering and distinctly human neurosis that without a crown or title, we are not enough.

Five years ago, when I was hosting the game show *To Tell the Truth,* one of my guests was sitting on my couch before the show began. She was making her first appearance on national television and seemed a bit nervous. Since we were appearing together, I thought it might be wise to get together before the show to quietly get acquainted. Her name was Nana, and she had just been given the title of World's Ugliest Dog.

I didn't book the contestants for the show, and according to FCC rules couldn't have anything to do with their booking. So each guest and his or her story was always a surprise to me — especially this one.

The meeting in the dressing room, in all honesty, was not for the benefit of the dog. It was for me. I was the one feeling a bit uncomfortable. *How ugly was she?*

Nana sat on my couch, with a bit of a shiver that she didn't lose. She looked like no dog I have ever seen. I couldn't recognize even a hint of a known breed in her. She was small — maybe six pounds. Her two little goggled eyes were different colors. Her pointed little ears stuck straight up. Her coat was a frizz of several different textures, missing whole patches. She wasn't comfortable standing straight up because some deformity in one hip caused her to list a bit when she walked, which was consequently a sort of leftward-drifting movement.

I didn't want this experience to go unappreciated. I always brought Betty and Scoshi to the set to let them wander among the backstage staff who became their every-other-weekend television family. So I wanted them both to meet Nana.

Scoshi came in first and immediately, as alpha male, tried to pick a fight with her. It was a quick exit, but I assured Nana that no harm was meant, and that he obviously considered her a formidable foe despite her infirmities, hoping she would take heart in that. Betty came in next. It was like the meeting of kindred souls. They sniffed and licked. Two rescues built from salvaged parts shared a private moment.

Nana sat on my desk during the show. It was her owner who was actually the subject of the game, and our celebrity panel was asking questions trying to determine who she was among the two imposters. Had the panel looked closely at the dog, they could have zeroed in on the owner. Nana never took her eyes off of her. She just sat there on national television shivering, staring, and wondering what the big deal was.

Dogs, regardless of their breed, seem to have a pretty strong sense of themselves, and to pick up on it pretty quickly. It takes us a lot longer, and sometimes we never do. We often look outside ourselves for things to define us — titles, degrees, and accomplishments. We let our fashion speak louder than our ideas. We let the media shape our opinions rather than take the time to explore and express what we believe. We determine our value by our wealth, our car, and our zip code. We covet the thrill of a walk down the red carpet over the quiet of a walk in the woods.

In every instance, the "we" is me. I'm guilty on all counts, and you can rub my nose in it. For me, developing a healthy self-image was the most challenging element in building my character.

In my early years as an adult I was not a leader, but a follower. Everyone seemed stronger and smarter, sharper with the tongues, their minds, and their ideas. I was easily influenced by others because I thought everyone else had a better idea than I did. As much as I wanted to be a leader of others, in truth, I was not even a leader of myself.

It wasn't until I started doing what I was supposed to be doing that my image of myself improved. When I decided to become an actor I connected to a fundamental purpose in my life. It is so much easier to feel good about yourself when you are attached to a purpose.

As I reflect on this, I am watching Betty busily hunting the gardens in our backyard.

Her little black snout forages through the greenery and the flowers, searching for some new scent, some small, new sign of life that she can sniff, paw, and, ultimately, roll over on. It is a ritual that is extremely important to her, and it will take hours. When she is finished, when there are no more scents to discover, she will come back inside, lie down at my feet, and close her eyes, totally consumed by her sense of purpose.

I remember myself, too, at the ages of three and four, wandering along the thick hedgerow of rosebushes that separated our house in East Hartford from our neighbors'. It was the year before we moved to Natick, Massachusetts, and I had our dachshund, Taffy, and discovered the wonders of the pond. But I treated those rosebushes with the same fascination and respect. For hours I would walk carefully past each bush, each flower, and, ever so carefully, with an almost surgical skill, remove each and every Japanese beetle that would cling and consume the beautiful blooms. As quickly as I would remove them, more would appear. Sometimes there were so many they would clump together and cleave to each other, like little circus acts. I would collect them all in a large glass mayonnaise jar and permanently remove them from the damage they did. The next day another swarm would appear, as if in defiance of my exhaustive work the day before. It just deepened my commitment to my purpose as the Great Exterminator.

As a kid, it was easy to find a purpose and just as easy to discard one. One day the beetle jar disappeared, the hedgerow was gone, and it was replaced with a pond and a net to catch turtles. A dog, however, never strays from its sense of purpose. Years may pass, but a hound will always dig and a retriever will always fetch, and Betty, being a mix, will always do both. It's what makes them happy.

As we grow into adulthood it is important that we, too, find focus for our lives, whether it is a career, our children, our pets, a hobby, a project, or our faith — or a combination of these things. It is through our focus that we learn the quiet confidence that what we *are* is enough, that we need not look outside ourselves for validation. Although if someone pats us on the head or rubs our belly, that's nice, too. But no award or title or accessory can give you the quiet sense of completion that comes from a healthy self-image. That joy comes only from owning your own fur.

I have the companionship of dogs to continually remind me of that. From Best in Show to World's Ugliest, the titles come and go and seem blissfully unimportant. Only one thing remains constant: dogs like being dogs, and they like being the dogs they are.

I have yet to win a Best in Show, and so far I have been lucky enough to avoid being named World's Ugliest. I've received some small recognitions somewhere in between the two, and that is enough.

But maybe someday, though — and this is the power of my well-oiled imagination speaking now — I may know the thrill of walking down the red carpet to a waiting golden statuette. I wonder in that most telling of moments whether I'll have the courage of my convictions to offer these words of acceptance:

It was a chance for a warm bath, a new haircut, some great food, a run down the carpet, and a chance to mingle with my own. All in all, a pretty good day.

For that . . . I'd like to thank the Academy.

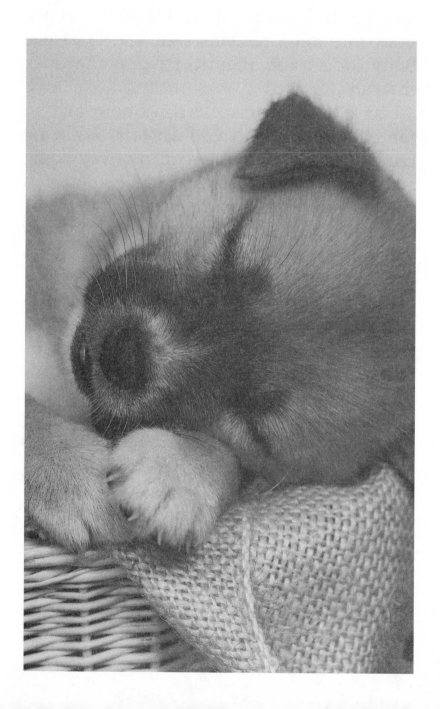

Never Miss a Nap

As I let my fingers tap quietly on the keys of my laptop, I feel pretty confident in saying that beyond all doubt there is a dog sleeping at my feet. I don't know which one it is because the screen obscures my view, but I sense with certainty the presence of a sleeping dog.

Yep. I'm right. It's Betty. She is stretched out on her side at the end of the bed. I should have known from the uneven pattern of her breathing. It's like she's snoring through a garden maze. Her leg twitches a bit, and she makes a slight whimpering sound, which means she's having a bad dream. Given her limited life experience, I'm guessing she's dreaming that she can't find her bowl in the kitchen. But she's deep asleep and halfway through her mid-morning nap.

There will be other naps during the day. This is just the first of many, and Scoshi will join her. There will be another at noon, one mid-afternoon. There'll be another after dinner and then one before bedtime. In between they'll squeeze in two meals, three or four walks, several chewies, an assault on a couple of toys, and many moments of wiggles and appreciation. But make no mistake — it's a lot about the napping. Scoshi and Betty are both napping machines.

Dogs love to sleep. I actually admire their ability to wander in and out of consciousness at whim. It's not something I can do with any consistency, nor something I can accomplish without the occasional sleep aid. Unlike my dogs, I've had a restless relationship with sleep ever since I can remember.

As a young child, I had to sleep with a blanket. It was called Bombie. I'm not sure whether I held a contest for the name, or whether it was just one of the favorites from my seven-word vocabulary, but Bombie and I had three good years of naps and nights together. Eventually Bombie surrendered to the wash and spin cycle, and what remained was only a small piece of one corner, which my mother attached to my pillow. Finally it disappeared altogether — about the same time I discovered my grandfather's lap.

All things become understandable in your

grandfather's lap, especially a nap. It was the point at which cherry pipe tobacco and weathered flannel mingled with a cherry lollipop and my Buster Brown shoes. It was the crossroad where wisdom met wonder. For the first four years of my life, I saw the world from this vantage. It passed by, page by page, in magazines with his thoughtful narration of every place and every page we ever journeyed. Mostly they were boating magazines.

Grandpa was a sage in the truest sense. He taught me my early love of the outdoors. He even built a boat in his attic once. It was a beautiful, handmade wooden motorboat, perfect for fishing on the Connecticut River. When the boat was finished, however, it was much too big to get out of the house by any normal means. It caused quite a stir in the neighborhood, and the boat in the attic became known as "George's folly." But they didn't realize Grandpa was a sage. He simply removed one side of the house and lowered the boat down, and then put the house back together all by himself.

I only had four years with him. Grandpa went to the hospital one day and didn't come back. I wasn't really sure what happened, but I remember how sad everyone was. After that, I remember visiting a small marble stone set in the ground of a large field. His name was on it, but he was nowhere around. I had lost Grandpa and his lap, my favorite vantage point, and I would have to learn to see the world in other ways.

I responded by embracing Grandma more. I had always loved her; I just loved Grandpa more, because he had the lap and the boating magazines. In his absence, though, she would become my favorite, and I would visit her on weekends in nearby Connecticut anytime my parents would let me.

But Grandma was different from Grandpa. She loved me dearly, and I loved the pancakes, tomato soup, grilled cheese sandwiches, and spaghetti. You couldn't beat the cuisine; she only cooked the things I liked. I also loved just hanging out with her. But it was different from how it had been hanging out in Grandpa's lap. Grandma didn't fish, she didn't know about boats, and she didn't have any magazines. While my Grandpa liked to do things, Grandma liked to nap.

Actually, Grandma was a professional napper. She could nap anytime and anywhere. She could nap at home or at our house, which for her was simply an "away game." When she would nap, she wanted you to nap with her. I later in life learned that misery loves company, but here, early on, I learned that inactivity does, too.

By four, though, I was mobile and I had reached the anti-napping age. Napping was for babies, and apparently, also for grand-mothers. In my young opinion, a nap inter-rupted and ruined the best part of the day — the middle part — when there was stuff to do. Plus, Grandma snored, which made napping not only unappealing, but impos-sible.

So I looked for other things to do while Grandma snored away a few hours each afternoon. One day her neighbor across the street invited me over to play with her son, who was about the same age. She had filled a plastic pool with water and invited me over to splash around with him. The only problem was I didn't have a swimsuit. So I woke Grandma from her nap to explain the invitation and my dilemma. I'm guessing I interrupted her in deep sleep because her solution revealed some clouded judgment.

Grandma reminded me that I had left a pair of underwear on my last visit two weeks earlier, and that I should wear them as a suit. Good idea, except I wasn't there two weeks ago. My older sister, Carol, was. She had left a pair of her 1959, fashionable and frilly young girl's underpants at Grandma's house during her last stay. In her grogginess, however, Grandma was now confusing the two of us and our underthings. The more I resisted, the more she insisted. Pretty soon after, when the fairy dust settled, Grandma returned to her nap. The front door opened, and I began the long walk of shame across the street to play with a kid I barely knew, and to sit in a little plastic pool in a pair of frilly girl's underpants. I sat there trying to deny that I was wearing girl's panties, but I jumped ship on that argument quickly and decided my energy was better spent splashing him and trying to convince a five-year-old that I wasn't a cross-dresser. Meanwhile, Grandma napped, and I never bothered to tell her about the consequences of her confusion.

Then I became not just against the notion of napping, I turned against sleep in general. For a while it seemed my sole desire in life was to stretch my bedtime later and later each night. It was as if I had realized that something wonderful was going to happen late at night. Older people knew it, but weren't letting the young people in on it. The later you stayed up the more fun it was going to be.

My father took me to a Red Sox game at

Fenway Park in Boston during Ted Williams's final season in 1960. I was five years old then. The splendor of a twilight game under the hallowed arches of Fenway in the presence of one of the best to ever play the game was great, but somehow small in light of the fact that I was going to get to stay up past midnight. I kept asking my father what time it was as each inning ticked by. When the game ended he put me in the backseat of the car for the half-hour trip back home, and I instructed him to tell me when midnight struck. I was only fifteen minutes away from the twelve o'clock milestone. At the stroke of midnight, he looked in the rearview mirror and I was fast asleep. A night that held so much promise went unfulfilled.

Growing up, for me, required a lot of staying up. I think I reached adulthood the night I could stay up as late as my parents. I would push the limits of my high school curfews an hour or two just to get the dangerous feeling that I was living on the other side of the night. The hours got later in college because, for the first time, I was living away from home, and I alone was responsible for my bedtime. An all-nighter became a way to study and a way to party; and breakfast became the perfect end to a perfect evening.

How ironic it was, though, that once I was asleep, I didn't want to wake up. In the morning you couldn't get me out of bed. As a kid, I'd actually set my alarm for seven-thirty on Saturday mornings, so I could wake up, turn it off, and enjoy the feeling of being able to drift back to sleep.

I don't know what age it finally occurred to me that sleep was a necessary part of human survival; that the body needs to rejuvenate. I suspect, though, it wasn't the common medical sense of it all that pushed me to the point of moderation. It was a conclusion reached after years of experience that nothing constructive ever occurs after midnight.

Getting a good night's sleep is one thing, but napping is quite another. By my thirties, I did develop a more mature habit of sleeping at a more mature time of the evening, but taking naps was still a sensitive point.

The central issue, really, is one of control. People like me, who don't like to appear out of control, have trouble admitting they are tired and need to nap. I'd drive a car well into the night, bleary-eyed before I'd let someone else take the wheel or pull over to close my eyes for a moment — an inherently dangerous extreme. If someone caught me dozing, my instinct was to apologize, "I'm sorry, I just shut my eyes for a moment." If someone telephoned when I was halfway through forty winks, I'd never answer with sleep in my voice. Never let 'em see you sweat; never let 'em know you nap.

Napping is an act of vulnerability. It is an acceptance of our fragility as humans; that we need to replenish ourselves; that we are not wholly complete. It gives the heart muscle a chance to rebuild, the cells a chance to wash and repair, and a chance for the hormonal flow in our bodies to rebalance.

Betty and Scoshi need no invitation to nap. When they are tired they curl up and close their eyes. They can't face a day full of walks and toys without sufficient rest. They know it and they've always known it. From the moment Mom drops the litter, dogs become masters of their own bedtimes and all the naps in between. Sleep isn't an issue of control for dogs. It isn't an issue of accepting their frailty. Dogs sleep because they're tired.

My wife, like the dogs, is a napper. So I have had to surrender my resistance to the majority. We have taken up a tradition, the Sunday Afternoon Nap. We all curl up in a cluster — the dogs, my wife, and I — and doze. I have come to enjoy this time together as a quiet punctuation point to a busy week. For an hour we gather to refresh and renew. For an hour I can put my arms around my family. For an hour I am out of control. For an hour I feel the vulnerability of what it means to be human and fragile.

And I haven't felt that vulnerable since I sat in a plastic pool wearing my sister's underwear.

You Are Only the Size You Think You Are

Good fences are supposed to make good neighbors. In between our house in Los Angeles and our neighbors' is one helluva fence.

Chain-link fences like this one dot the Hollywood Hills. It is twelve feet high and set three feet into the ground. This one was designed with only the best of intentions — not to keep neighbors apart, or to keep intruders out, although it certainly does both. It was put up to bar access to coyotes who wander the hills in packs, preying on pets and property values. While coyotes can leap tall fences in a single bound, apparently none has yet to break the twelve-foot mark.

The fence keeps the coyotes in check. While it also keeps me from any meaningful contact with my neighbors, it does not prevent Scoshi from his daily confrontation with his. For several years we lived next door to people I rarely saw, but Scoshi lived next door to two enormous Doberman pinschers. Every morning after breakfast he would head out to bang heads at the fence with these two behemoths. The moment I opened the door for him, he hit full stride. He needed no words of encouragement, no prep for battle. By the time he reached the side garden, they were already gathered at the fence links waiting for him. His last step was a four-foot leap onto the fence to let them know that he'd arrived.

When he's in good voice, Scoshi possesses the bark of seven dogs. The Dobermans had deep, rich woofs, and all three combine in a chorus that filled the Hollywood Hills with the kind of cacophony that you'd expect at a Stones concert.

This was an argument about turf. They were reminding each other where the boundary began and ended. The steel links kept the fight fair, although Scoshi's snout was narrow enough to fit through the links and deliver a couple of harmless nibbles. The dirt would fly, and the fence would rattle from the weight of three dogs hurling themselves against it.

The Great Border Dispute started before Betty was in residence with us. She strayed her way into our lives about a year later.

While it is not her temperament to be aggressive, she quickly joined ranks at the fence each morning as a show of family unity and to protect her new brother.

Then the neighbors moved, where or why I don't know. One sunny morning I simply noticed that the Dobermans had been replaced by a Saint Bernard and a large chocolate Labrador retriever. (Large dogs must have been part of the contingency for the sale of the property.) The new version of the Great Border Dispute took pretty much the same shape, except that the Saint Bernard now added a healthy dose of saliva to the mix, which elevated the action to mud wrestling.

The Great Border Dispute had all the posturing of a good schoolyard rumble. Mostly, though, the altercation seemed to be about respect. The dogs were drawing the same lines between them that we do as humans, except that we do it more indirectly with property lines, lawsuits, zoning commissions, and co-op boards. Instead of throwing ourselves against the fence, we unleash our attorneys. We let them scrap it out for us until we reach the point when the barking and the taunting no longer make sense. Then we reach some level of settlement that makes everyone look like they've retained some turf and self-respect.

What is different about the dogs' daily standoff and our so-called reasonable confrontations is that to us, size matters. We normally assess both the bulk and the strength of our opponents before we attempt to draw first blood. Dogs don't realize how big or small they are or what that means. Our neighbors' dogs outsized and outweighed Betty and Scoshi by a multiple of four. It was the equivalent of my confronting a twenty-four-foot man weighing a quarter of a ton as a daily exercise.

I actually did that once as a youngster, and it made quite an impression.

At the age of twelve I realized I was trapped in a body that wasn't evolving at a pace with the rest of my species. I was tall and gangly, not much muscle. I was the kind of jungle specimen that could be easily eliminated if nature ever decided to thin the herd.

My lack of physical stature was making school especially perilous. Practically overnight, the focus of recess went from playing catch to a warring pack of jackals vying for territory (thanks to the swirl of our seventh-grade hormones). Every day, it seemed someone was butting heads with someone else, and rather than go mano a mano, the boys in my class organized in packs. It was a time of real tension for me because every now and then my scent would cross their path when they were looking for easy prey. So I had to learn to be quick with the tongue and polish my wit to diffuse a gathering storm. And it was always at the expense of my self-respect. It was like pleading for your life with a grizzly by trying to convince him that you don't taste good.

I realized that I had to do something to ensure my survival. So I enrolled in judo classes, where I learned to flip and trip my way through physical confrontations. It soon occurred to me, however, that this art left me at a distinct disadvantage, because to flip someone, you had to get pretty close. In fact, close enough to give them a chance to pummel you before you turned gravity against them. So I looked for something else — and happened upon karate. Karate, you see, was perfect for me. In my mind, kicking and chopping trumped flipping and tripping any day. I could work my martial hocus-pocus from the safe distance of my extra-long arms and legs.

Within weeks, karate became my passion. I took classes at the local YMCA in Connecticut, and when I could finally convince my parents that I needed to move to a more legitimate level of training, they drove me on Saturdays to a class at an actual karate studio. I saved every penny I could to buy a *gi*, an official karate outfit. The basement of our home became my secret training camp, my dojo, made up mostly of cushions from the couches.

One night my father, who was a doctor, came home from a particularly long day to find me in the living room, dressed in my *gi*. I just *had* to show him what I had learned in training that day. He barely had time to take off his coat and drop his black doctor's bag before I dragged him into position in the living room and directed him to approach me menacingly as though he wanted to strangle me (something I'm sure I'd given him reason to consider before). As he started his approach, I assumed The Stance — a posture of poise and preparation, where the body is in perfect fluid balance, ready to strike. With his arms aimed right for my throat, in a flash I thrust my arms straight up through them, separating his arms and sending them flailing to either side. Then I kicked him in the balls.

I had never actually heard someone make the noise my father did then. It was a kind of deep whimper as the air left his body in one dramatic gasp. His eyes shut tight. He disappeared quickly, went upstairs to his room, and didn't come down until the following morning.

I got my chance to test my mettle (on someone other than my poor dad) one Saturday afternoon in the most surprising of situations. The local junior high school was sponsoring a carnival complete with rides and midway games. It drew most of the town's youth that day, as there was nowhere else to be. I went there by myself, and walked around the carnival for most of the afternoon. Late in the day, as I started for home, I came around the front of the school, past the playground area where the swings and monkey bars were. Two girls were drifting back and forth on the swings talking. I had never seen them before. They were older girls — thirteen, maybe thirteen and a half, which made them instantly attractive. One had hazel eyes and long, beautiful, sandy-colored hair that looked as though it was ironed straight. The other girl was wearing the newest fashion rage — cutoff jeans. This made them more than attractive. This made them knockouts. But they were also in a predicament. Two boys were standing nearby, leaning against the steel supports, teasing them. The girls didn't like this, I quickly surmised, and they clearly wanted to be left alone.

I had never seen the two boys before, either. They were about the same age as the girls, both were bigger than me and looked as though they played on every athletic team that I'd been cut from, and they actually filled out the jeans and T-shirts they were wearing. None of this mattered to me. I had trained for this moment. I was a young Don Quixote, ready now to topple windmills and teasing giants alike.

A situation like the one about to brew begged for the right words.

"Why don't you just leave the girls alone?" I asked in the deepest voice I could muster, like someone had just pinned me sheriff.

That's what I led with — pure poetry. Thinking back now with the wisdom of years, I'm surprised one of the girls didn't stand up and slap me.

The stupidity of my question was like chumming the waters with blood. The two boys instantly turned their attention from the girls and furrowed their brows in my direction. The girls used this moment to make a quick and quiet exit. Now it was just Me and Them.

I made the same sound as I hit the chain-link school fence that Scoshi did hitting the fence to attack the neighbors' dogs some thirty years later. The only difference being that Scoshi was proactive, and I was recoiling from something that hit me so fast I didn't know what it was. I still don't.

"So you're a tough guy, huh?" I'm guessing they asked this rhetorically.

The concussion of hitting the fence with most of my face woke up the six-week warrior within me. What followed was only the purest form of instinct, free of thought. I shook the blur from my eyes and stared into the space between them. My hands raised slightly, the legs bent softly, the back flattened, and my shoulders dropped. I had assumed The Stance.

They say it's the eye of the tiger that kills its prey. The intensity in the stare burns like a laser through the heart of the victim. It paralyzes it with fear. I swayed deliberately from foot to foot, my hands moved in slow circles. I felt the power of perfect balance, the charge of adrenaline. I was prepared to strike.

But not for what happened. I was not prepared for the laughter. The more I shifted my weight and swirled my hands, the harder they laughed. They started to mimic my moves, slashing the air with their hands, shouting like Charlie Chan, "Whoo, haah!"

I continued The Stance while they mocked and danced around me. I suddenly felt like I was watching the sacred history of the martial warrior disappear before me like air from a balloon. They continued to laugh as they slapped each other on the back, still chopping and kicking. They turned and went on their way.

The sense of relief was mixed with a sense of disgrace. I had probably escaped the beating of my life, and I was grateful for that. But I realized that, with all the training, the outfit, the preoccupation, I posed no threat. I was merely entertainment.

I didn't continue in martial arts. I bought an electric guitar instead, and the warrior quickly turned poet. The wind had been taken out of my sails. If I learned anything from the experience, it was probably to wait my turn for puberty to fill me out, and to stop looking for damsels in distress.

Fortunately, my dogs have taught me more about confrontation than I ever could learn on my own. We are only the size we think we are. No one can make you seem small — you have to do that for them.

What makes us shrink in size and shrink away from confrontation is not having the quiet confidence of our convictions. It is our faith in what we believe that gives us the power to express ourselves. My wife's parents have a tiny Yorkshire terrier named Chloe who struts around the streets of Vail, Colorado, like she's the elected mayor. She'll go face-to-face with any dog of any size, but for most of her public life she walks as if she were headlining her own parade. Perhaps this is what I missed in the message of martial arts. I used karate to shop for a cause, rather than let it fill me with the confidence of who I am and give me the strength and the wisdom to defend what I believe.

Dogs seem to confront naturally, humans confront conditionally. What makes this observation more interesting is that dogs' confrontations are physical; rarely are adult confrontations anything but verbal. As we pass the age of our schoolyard scuffles, most of our lashing is done with our tongues, not our fists. Because of this we have the figurative cushion of the chain-link fence between our adversaries and us. A battle of words doesn't break us or bruise us — not physically, at least. There are no sticks and stones. If there are — get a good lawyer.

We define ourselves not only by what we say yes to, but also by the courage to say no. We often agree with the status quo rather than expend the energy it takes to evoke change. Yet, confrontation is a healthy and necessary part of sharing space on this planet. It is the reason we put up fences in the first place. They are the borders defining who we are and where we are. All through our lives we have to continually define our fences to the world around us. Sometimes it means we have to stand at the fence, that white line of who and what we are — and imagine the giant within us.

IF YOU'RE HAPPY AND YOU KNOW IT WAG YOUR TAIL

When it's working properly, New York City is a well-oiled machine. You have your choice of cabs, a soft breeze has cleaned the air, the Yanks and the Mets have both won, a subway car stops right at your feet — a *Daily News* is folded up and lying near your choice of seats. The elevator door is open and waiting on the ground floor with no one inside, and you arrive where you need to be with nothing stuck to the bottom of your shoes.

When it's broken, however, New York is a labyrinth of inconvenience. If it's raining, all the umbrellas go up, which immediately triples the pedestrian population. If it's windy, the city becomes a swirl of newspaper, trash, and toupees. One service on strike affects them all. Every cab in your direction is off-duty. Anything you have thought of doing, ten people have thought of before you, at exactly the same time. The line always seems to be longer in front of you than behind.

So you have to assess how the city is functioning on the day you need to make a trip as important as the one to my afternoon meeting with Clayton.

I was meeting Clayton at the Morgan Stanley Children's Hospital of New York–Presbyterian, on Broadway and 166th Street in upper Manhattan. The meeting was my idea, and it had been difficult to arrange time alone with him, given the complexities of scheduling in the demanding world of patient care.

I was coming from Union Square, in the lower part of the city. It was a beautiful, warm winter's day. The Mets and the Yanks were not even in spring training yet, but Manhattan seemed otherwise to be in perfect working order that day, so I decided to test the subway for the underground journey of 150 blocks. Sure enough, as I entered the station, the uptown express train stopped right in front of me. Someone had left a copy of the *Daily News* on the empty bench seat of my subway car, so I unfolded the paper, crossed my legs, and settled in for a long winter's ride.

As we traveled north the car began to slowly fill with people, which I barely noticed, since I was busy reading the discarded-but-happily-received-by-me copy of the *Daily News*. Perhaps it is because that particular paper seems to align with my oh-so-casual knowledge of world events that I found myself deeply engrossed in an article on the radical jump in Manhattan real estate values. As the subway train pulled into the 168th Street station, I barely noticed our arrival before the doors opened. I jumped up so as not to miss my stop, and I felt a flash of panic mixed with pins and needles — my leg was asleep. Dead asleep. In fact, it was sleeping so deeply that I couldn't even feel it as I used both hands to uncross it. My leg hit the floor of the car with a kind of cadaverous thump, and I quickly realized as I tried but couldn't stand on it that I wasn't going to make that exit. I sat back down and the doors shut as we slowly headed out of the station. I looked at my watch and I realized I was going to be late for my meeting with Clayton.

We were at the final stop in Manhattan, just shy of the Bronx, before I was able to stomp enough circulation back into my gimpy leg to render it useful again. I got off the train and paid another fare to catch the subway heading back downtown.

I was twenty minutes late when I arrived

at the hospital. Hustling up the winding ramp toward the lobby, I found Clayton waiting for me. I had never met him before, but he was kind of easy to spot — he was the only dog in the hospital lobby.

Clayton is a ten-year-old black Labrador retriever. He wears a hospital photo identification badge attached to his collar to indicate his official clearance as part of the fourteen-member dog therapy team. The team is part of a program called Angel on a Leash, funded by the Westminster Kennel Club. It trains dogs to interact with patients of all ages and medical conditions. When I first heard of this program years earlier, I was immediately taken by the genius of it and also by its inherent complications. Dogs don't seem to mix with sterile environments. So I wanted to shadow him on a day's visit.

I was also interested in the possibility that this might be a wonderful opportunity for Betty, who, because she is one of the gentlest creatures on Earth, might be a good candidate for a therapy dog.

Every dog in the program goes through rigorous training and certification. They must respond to voice commands and demonstrate a calm disposition in a variety of social situations. They are bathed thoroughly before each visit and sit on a special sheet when they are on a patient's bed. They can't lick, and the patient's hands are washed after the visit.

Sometimes they are there for a simple feel-good visit. Other times it will be to help a patient through a session of physical therapy. The need to reach and pet a dog can strengthen and stretch muscles that are atrophied or undeveloped. At more critical moments, the calming presence of a dog like Clayton has allowed reluctant victims to reveal instances of physical and sexual abuse and helped the chronically ill through bouts of depression.

He was trained originally as a Seeing Eye dog for the blind, which, I suppose, earns him the high respect of marine boot camp from other dogs. For minor medical reasons he was honorably discharged to his present post. He bears the unmistakable softness in the eyes and the constant wag of the tail that is so characteristic of his breed.

As further evidence of his earlier training, Clayton moves with thoughtful concern for the pace of his handler, Greer Griffith. Greer not only volunteers her time for therapy dog visits, but spends time with the Delta Society, the body that trains and certifies the dogs. She possesses a wonderful blend of gentleness and self-assurance that helps her communicate so easily with the pediatric patients and also keep a dog in line with policy and procedure.

On the first floor we visited, I was struck by an odd mix of sensations. Bright sun shone through the windows, framing a spectacular vista of the full stretch of Manhattan. The interior walls featured full-length, hand-painted murals of classic children's stories, each with an inspired verse of hope and promise. But even cartoons and colors could not mask the seriousness of the place. We were in the children's cancer unit. From any point you could look into a doorway and see a child with no hair. At a glance, it was often impossible to tell if they were girls or boys. This is a savage truth of cancer therapy, and the reality of it made me terribly uneasy.

Clayton, however, seemed right at home. Dogs treat sickness and health with equal value. His tail continued to wag as we began our rounds. The response to Clayton was quite remarkable — a bit like a nun at a football game. All eyes settled on Clayton. Every conversation stopped, every pen and every medical chart dropped. People paused as he walked by. Clayton moved like a dog but was greeted with the fondness of a saint carried in a festival.

Clayton knew to stop at each door. Before entering, his handler would look in to see if a parent was there to give permission for a visit. Sadly, some kids are simply too sick to see anyone.

The first door we came to named a little boy, Raphael, on the chart. He was sitting straight up in his bed. He had no hair, no eyebrows. No one was in the room with him, but because of the severity of his condition we couldn't enter either. So Greer tapped on the glass and Raphael peered over through the metal side supports of his bed. Clayton, ready for his close-up, stood tall and Greer raised his paw to wave hello through the window. The boy waved back and smiled. Clayton and Raphael continued to wave at each other for a good minute.

The boy's smile was not one of surprise as much as one of serenity, as though in this child's memory, dogs had waved at him before. Greer reached into her pocket for a small plastic bag, which held wallet-size pictures of Clayton. She handed one to one of the nurses who stood by watching. The nurse opened the door, walked in, and presented the child with the picture. She left the room as the child stared at the photograph. Then, with all of us gathered with Clayton at the door, he brought the picture to his lips and gently kissed it — and the breath left every one of us.

Farther down the hall we entered a room where Louise, a little girl of about ten, was lying in her bed. Her mother, who was seated nearby, gave permission for a visit. The girl had lost not only all of her hair, but her expression as well. She stared blankly at a video game, which she was playing alone; a drawn look in her eyes indicated to me that she'd been here a while and one moment slipped, without notice, into the next. When Clayton entered the room, however, she came to life.

Louise sat straight up in the bed and put both of her hands to her face, to cover the little sound she made. One joyful gasp became another as Clayton walked right up to the side of her bed and sat, waiting for instructions. A sheet was spread out on Louise's bed. Clayton jumped up to lie at her feet and she began petting him.

How interesting it is that unconsciously we relate to animals, especially dogs, by stroking them. It is certainly not something we would do casually with another human being. Dogs, without cause, seem to break down the barriers to intimacy.

As Louise petted Clayton, she started to

talk about how much she missed her dog at home. Clayton enjoyed every stroke of her hand and quietly laid his head by her knees. In the reverie of her time with Clayton, she continued to talk in a stream of consciousness about things that seemed important at the moment. Much of the conversation came at the urging of Greer, who had a deep sense of the healing power of simple conversation. As Louise talked, she shifted in bed so as to better pet the dog. Every inch closer she moved to the dog, the video game was further and further away.

A few minutes later, Clayton was sitting with an eighteen-year-old named Jose. He was petting him and talking about how much he loved to design sneakers. A well-known shoe company had paid him for a couple of his designs just before he got very sick. My heart hurt from the sound of resignation in his voice. Framed in bed by tubes and wires, being fed and monitored by the latest technology, and all Jose wanted to do was make sneakers. As he talked, he continued to pet Clayton.

Being an actor has spoiled me with conclusions. Stories in film and on stage have an arc — a beginning, middle, and, if they're well-told, a surprise ending. Not that day. There was no conclusion to any of these stories. Clayton was not curing the cancer — although he was, for a few moments, restoring the joy in these children's lives.

I left Clayton in the hospital lobby after several hours of bedside visits. He seemed as cheerful then as when I first met him hours earlier, and peacefully unaware of the moments of happiness he had brought to people in so much need. I knelt down in front of him to give his face a good rub. The tenderness of his gaze said it all. He needed no thanks; he was just doing what any dog would do.

That's the truth about dogs. They don't know what they do, yet they do great things. They sit in silent vigil by our sides and with so little effort bring so much joy. By simply being there, they evoke all the things that are truly good in life — laughter, love, and intimacy. And they do it all with the wag of a tail.

People don't have tails — we have smiles, which, when used appropriately, communicate the same goodness in life. That was the message I left with.

I decided to give the subway another shot; the city still seemed well-oiled. Sure enough, a train appeared in moments and I found a seat, but no discarded newspaper this time.

The train was now filling with the end-of-the-day crowd, so there was no room to cross my legs. So I just sat there, looking up and down the car. Most people were staring straight ahead, focusing on nothing in particular. Most looked as though they wished they were someplace — anywhere — else. Their stares seemed like masks of resignation, remarkably similar to the stares of the children I had just left, who also wished to be someplace else. At that moment it occurred to me that, as much as we try to appear to the contrary, we humans are not well-oiled machines. To some degree, we are all broken. What connects us to each other is our willingness to accept that frailty in each other, to accept that we all need. That connection starts with a smile. A smile is like the wag of a tail that communicates at a deep and disarming level and says, "I understand."

So I tried to smile a bit as the train continued on its path downtown. Not the flashy, Hollywood grin on my press photo, but a simple, heartfelt one that reflected the meaning of the two hours I had spent with Clayton. I didn't force it on anyone, but instead let it creep gently across my face as someone's blank stare locked mine. The unexpectedness of the gesture caused some to turn away; some seemed to not notice at all. Some broke rank and smiled back, but quickly turned their gaze away as though it revealed too much. Maybe it would have been a simpler exercise if I'd had a tail to wag.

One little girl, about four, kept turning back to me, trying to figure out *why* I was smiling. She appeared to ponder it for a while before her eyes began to twinkle. A young mother entered the car trying to negotiate a folded-up stroller, an infant, and two young children. When she got settled, she took a deep breath and let out a small sigh. It was easy to see she had reached the limit of what she could handle. When she looked across the aisle, I smiled enough to let her know that I appreciated her difficulty. She smiled back and it seemed to lighten her burden. It lightened mine as well.

I would have missed these moments if I had simply crossed my legs and buried my head in another discarded newspaper. I would have missed the intimacy of the unexpected smile from across the aisle. I would have sat there, my affect as deeply numbed as my crossed leg had been when I arrived. Instead, I felt a strange, wonderful connection. It was a connection to a deeper sense of what's important. Like Clayton, I wasn't there to cure, but to offer comfort. It is a wonderful irony that in our empathy for others, we feel healthier ourselves.

Betty and Scoshi were at the door to greet me when I arrived home an hour later. As the door slowly opened, their little faces appeared in the crack, one above the other. As I walked in, they circled me, sniffing in a frenzy, sussing out the unusual blend of Clayton and the New York City subway. Soon all was calm. They'd come to terms with the fact that I'd been with another dog, and they sat beside my wife and me on the couch as I talked about the events of the day.

As I was talking about what the hospital visit meant to me, I realized I was petting Betty as she lay next to me. Scoshi was quietly snoring from his perch atop the sofa. I paused to hold a memory of the moment, and smiled softly at my wife as I realized that the two of them were simply picking up where Clayton had left off.

EVERY DAY IS A STRETCH

There is a joke among mushers, the dogsledders who live in the beautiful expanse of Alaska, that goes like this: If you're not the lead dog, the view never changes. The joke is also a brutal but honest way to describe the three months of my life on the high school cross-country running team.

I'll back up a bit (which is another way to describe my running ability). I stumbled into running cross-country as a way to avoid two other sports — football and soccer. My high school, an all-boys' school, mandated sports for all students. I had already proven myself to be one of the worst players in the history of the school to suit up for football, so I had to move on. A day at football practice was a slow death march for me.

Soccer was less violent, but also afforded less padding. It also struck me as a bit pointless. You kick the ball and sprint in four different directions for two hours, and still there's a good chance you'll end up in a tie.

But our school had never fielded a cross-country team before, so it started one my junior year. A new sport, I thought, perfect. No expectations, no school records to live up to. We could be individually and collectively mediocre, and no one would care, as there was nothing to compare us to. We also had no coaching. Well, technically, we had a coach, but he was as new to long-distance running as the twenty of us who had signed up to be the team.

The first day of practice Coach Doyle presented us with our running shoes. Track shoes. To be exact, they were sprinter's shoes, with only the slightest padding under the toes and the ball of the foot — but nowhere else. We soon learned that you couldn't run on the balls of your feet for very long. They were made for running distances of a hundred yards, not, say, three and a half miles. It was as opposite to the purpose as sticking a fishhook through your lip and throwing the rod and reel into the water. It wasn't until our first running meet, when the coach of the other team quietly pulled Coach Doyle aside, that we were told we all had the wrong shoes.

It hardly mattered to me. I could have discarded the shoes and run in the shoe boxes, I was that inept. Our first practice was a three-mile run to the local reservoir and back. I was out of breath by the first quarter-mile and fell so far behind that it never made sense to run the whole distance. As everybody passed me on the way back, I just joined the end of the line that was running home.

The situation didn't improve much. Over the next three weeks the running got a little easier, but I had no endurance. You can only imagine how well I did in our running meets. I came in last in almost every race. Occasionally, I'd glance over my shoulder and see someone from the other team behind me. Out of empathy I actually felt as though I should stop and wait for him to catch up. Finishing last and tying for last were not separate glories.

It never occurred to me that distance running required stretching, both before and after training. I had the flexibility of a potato chip. After our first team run of three miles, my muscles were so bound up and my calves so cramped that I had to sit on the stairs at home and inch up, one step at a time, on my butt to get to my room. The next morning my legs were frozen straight. My knees wouldn't bend. I had to lift my hips and throw my legs forward to move. I walked like I was wearing a dirty diaper.

It was a clearly frustrating point in my young life. I got pummeled on the football field and now I was the runt of the litter on the cross-country team. I hated running, and I was beginning to hate sports in general.

Curiously, we had an English springer spaniel at this time, named Ding, who loved to run. We had adopted her from a show breeder when she was six months old, and she came to us with the rather odd, AKC-registered name Champion Tara's Jingle. "Ding" seemed to fit much better. She was perhaps the most beautiful dog I have seen to this day. Dappled with black and white markings and a perfectly formed head, she represented the best qualities of her breed. Her soft, dark eyes were always gentle but alert. Her parents were both breed champions. The "Champion" in front of her registered name celebrated her lineage. I remember being very impressed with this, like we had adopted royalty.

Ding was a bit smaller than most of her breed. She also had some bladder control issues that caused her to squat and pee at the sound of a deep voice, most notably my father's. That habit, combined with her more compact build, brought the possibilities of a promising dog show career to a skidding halt.

As I said, there was one thing that Ding loved to do that I did not. She loved to run. By the nature of the breed, English springer spaniels are both water dogs and hunting retrievers. Their ground speed is extraordinary, and this gives them an advantage to flush small game and birds in open field runs. Watching Ding gather speed and reach full stride was to experience not the sport, but the true beauty of running. Her back would flatten and lower as she dug through each step, her front legs at full extension. She would also do something characteristic of her breed — at top speed she would spring forward. Her black, pendant ears would fly straight out and flatten. When she reached the peak of her leap, she would just *hang* there. She would float for a second, suspending time and gravity, and then return to the earth in full stride. Not only was she beautiful, she moved with a grace and elegance that I had never before seen.

Ding was bred to run. Clearly I was not. But one particular night after supper, I was throwing a tennis ball for Ding to retrieve in the backyard. True to her bird-dog breeding, retrieving an old tennis ball thrown deep into the woods was, for her, about as good as life gets. She'd race to the edge of the woods, leap, and hang in the air. She'd disappear into the lush, green underbrush for only a moment, and then leap again when she found the prize. She'd race back to you, drop a soggy yellow tennis ball at your feet, then rear up and bark until you threw it again. And again.

This one particular night came after another stunning last-place finish for me earlier that afternoon at a special five-school meet in Springfield, Massachusetts. It's bad enough to finish last against one team, but when there isn't anybody in *five* schools that is slower than you, you feel that the universe has drawn a slow, deep breath to deliver a decisive and conclusive judgment — you *really* suck.

I was lost in the embarrassment of the day as I was throwing Ding her now nearly masticated tennis ball for what must have been the 200th time, when a thought hit me. I mean, *hit me,* like a slap in the face. What if, I thought, I pretended, just for a day — for one practice — that I could run like Ding, free of thought, racing for the pure enjoyment of running? What would it feel like to sprint, without tiring, at the head of the pack? I was an actor, after all; I should be able to imagine myself as the greatest runner of all time, "Ding-for-a-Day" O'Hurley.

I couldn't wait to get to cross-country practice the next day; it was like I had awakened with a new sense of purpose. We were working on a flat gravel track that afternoon, rather than running a field course. I don't remember the technical reason for doing so, but it didn't matter much to me. I went to the track feeling dangerous, like a man with nothing to lose, a man with a score to settle. I was more relaxed than I had ever been. I talked to no one, lest anyone break my focus. In my head, I made up a theme song, a kind of trumpeted anthem that would close the Olympic Games. I hummed it silently to myself to accompany my swagger as I waited for the team to assemble at the starting line. I even introduced myself over an imaginary public address system and acknowledged the phantom roar of the crowd with a thoughtful nod of my head as I moved up to the white lime mark on the track. Coach Doyle set the mark and fired the gun.

I will remember those first ten steps for the rest of my life. They were long and digging. The gray gravel beneath my feet crunched with a sound I'd never heard before. These ten steps set me out in front of the pack for the first time in my life. It was the view the dogsled mushers joked about. It was free and clear, and it was all I needed. From that moment on, I wasn't going to let anyone pass me. My mind and body were flushed with adrenaline. I felt every step connect with my core. I was running like Ding.

Coach Doyle was still at the starting line as we came around the turn to complete the first lap. I was still in front, digging with every step; the rest of the world was behind me. If I had given birth at that moment I wouldn't have seen more surprise on his face.

I led through the second lap unwilling to surrender the lead or the experience. In my head I was screaming my theme song, while an imaginary announcer mopped his brow and tore his tie off in excitement. Even the air that I was now sucking into my lungs had a different scent. It was air that no one had breathed before, with a fragrance that only the leader can enjoy.

By the end of the third lap, the halfway point of the three-mile run, the poetry of the moment gave way to trappings of physical law. The more elite runners of our team, who'd been pacing their run, began to stretch their strides and close the gap. As we passed Coach Doyle after the turn, my pace began to slacken, and the select group of Those Who Run Better slowly began to envelop me.

I wasn't done yet. After all, this was my fantasy, not theirs, and they hadn't seen my third act yet. In an instant, I simply changed my thinking. Instead of running alone out front, I would now run with the select group of Those Who Run Better, as proudly as if I was one of their own. If Ding could motivate herself to chase the same tennis ball two hundred times, then surely I could re-create some driving image to inspire me further.

I lasted two more laps with them, with one to go. By now my legs felt like the consistency of cottage cheese, my lungs were making a loud sucking sound, and my head was bobbing in a noticeable left-to-right pattern. In the final lap, the group moved on ahead, and I was left behind to follow, kind of like a rocket stage that had just been jettisoned. In their place, I found myself surrounded by the more common group of Those Who Ran Decently.

There I finished, in the precious middle of the pack, right in the meaty part of the bell curve. Not first, not last. That day someone else had to bear the view of being the final dog. I wouldn't be surprised if his life has been hell ever since.

The entire race took a little more than twenty-five minutes, but, to me, it seemed like a lifetime. Perhaps in some way, it was a lifetime. I had always been last, but now I knew what it felt like to be first. The experience was not lost on Coach Doyle, who couldn't congratulate me enough on my effort. I think I was still recovering from oxygen deprivation as I gurgled in response to his praise. I continued running on the team through the end of the fall season. I never won, but I was never last again.

More important, though, the lesson was not lost on me. I had been able to change my results by changing my thinking. If I ran like a failure it was because I thought like a failure. Ding ran as beautifully as she did because she loved to run.

Another lesson came from this, perhaps an even more enduring one. It is one that Ding and every dog ever since has shared with me. They stretch. All dogs do, young and old.

Now, Ding and I had obvious physical differences. She was sculpted with long, sinewy muscle. I was about as flexible as a pencil. Every morning, Ding would rise from sleep, stand tall on her haunches, and stretch her front legs and her neck as far forward as she could. (In yoga, it's called the Downward Dog, which I'm guessing they use without permission.) Then she'd give her head a shake to loosen the muscles of the neck and shoulders. Then she'd lie down on her back and roll from side to side to stretch the abdominals.

Who taught Ding to do this? Who sat her down and said, "Look, you're a dog; dogs run, so maybe you should stretch." Nobody. Puppies stretch from the first moment after their first nap, and they don't stop stretching for their entire lives. Today, Scoshi is a fifteen-year old Maltese, and he limps from arthritis like an old linebacker. Yet, every morning, he hops off the pillow on the bed and walks down past the spot where my wife is sleeping and does two minutes of doggy yoga.

Dogs understand their bodies because they are, by nature, physical creatures. They condition their bodies because they need them. Human beings do not. We are born with the flexibility to put our feet in our mouths. As infants we can be bent and shaped into any position. As youngsters we build our bodies for play and sports. When we reach adulthood, however, our physical nature seems to become less important to us. We become more cerebral and less physical. At the same time, gravity and age combine to slowly curve our bodies and shorten our muscles. One in three adults is obese after the age of twenty — not paunchy, but obese. By forty, only one in ten adults can touch their toes. The running and playing of our youth is replaced by a walk to the car and a tug on the seat belt, or a point and click of the mouse.

While dogs suffer from the same degenerative ailments like arthritis and circulatory problems that we do, rarely, if ever, do you hear of a dog pulling or tearing a muscle. They instinctively maintain their flexibility and consequently live far more active lives in their later years. At the age of fifteen (if you regard the seven-to-one ratio of human-to-dog years with any truth), Scoshi has passed the century mark. Yet every day he takes his sprightly walk down Broadway at a brisk clip, with a little limp, only a few steps behind Betty. When we've completed the night walk, I'll unhook their leashes on the elevator. As the doors open, I'll yell, "Where do we live? Where do we live?" and Betty will tear down the hall and disappear around two corners to search for the right door. Scoshi follows right behind, all one hundred dog-years of him, running as fast as he can. (If you're a dog, you can't beat finding your door for entertainment.) I don't know how many one-hundred-year-old men could keep pace with them.

I think Scoshi's attitude and ability has become my goal in life today. At the age of a hundred, I, too, want to be able to race down a hallway (with my wife in tow) and still find my door. I want to be an inexhaustible old man, chasing old tennis balls and golf balls alike. It no longer matters to me where I finish in the pack. Today, I set my pace on a treadmill, no longer concerned that the entire cross-country team is already on the bus, waiting for me to finish. It is no longer important *how* I run, but *that* I run, and enjoy the view.

That is the message from Ding and every dog that has crossed my path — that strength and speed may slowly disappear, but flexibility is enduring. That message has been lying at my feet all my life. I was simply too stiff to bend down and see it.

EPILOGUE

If Hallmark cards have taught us anything, it is that appreciation looks best in print. So it seems fitting to conclude these reflections with a word of thanks to Betty, Scoshi, Taffy, Ding, Reagan, and all the precious little creatures that have filled my life with love and inspired my life by living theirs with such innocence.

I think it is sadly true that most teachers who inspire us never get to see the fruits of what they sow. The lessons of today often find a deeper meaning further down the road, out of sight. I think it is also true that most teachers are unaware of when they are actually teaching, that the simplest words and actions can sometimes instruct and enlighten more than all the lectures one could ever hope to deliver.

At the same school that was the arena for my many athletic nightmares, the same school that was the backdrop for my romantic disappointments, there was a teacher named Mr. Driscoll, who taught English. He always presented himself keenly dressed in a wool blazer, flannel slacks, and tie, like a gentlemen's gentleman. He would make us read aloud the literature that he taught, especially the plays. With each new assignment, he would hand out roles to each of us, including the women's roles — although all were performed by a roomful of young teenage boys. Nobody tried to give any sort of characterization to what they read. No one delivered any meaning to the words they spoke, or raised their voices beyond a colorless monotone. No one except me. I was an actor, after all (at least in my head), and that small classroom in Connecticut was as important a stage as any. I waxed with each line and savored every bit of nuance that I could bring.

At the end of one particular class on a late February afternoon, after we had just finished reading the classic comedy *Life with Father,* Mr. Driscoll asked me to remain behind. I remember the icy feeling of anxiety mixed with the low winter light coming through the classroom windows, as my classmates all rose and left the room. After a moment of silence, Mr. Driscoll looked up from his desk and told me how much he enjoyed the effort I put into reading the plays. He said that I was very good and that I should consider auditioning for the next school play. Then, with the same casual matter-of-factness, he dismissed me.

I would remember that moment for the rest of my life. It was the first time anyone had ever encouraged me to be an actor, and the last time anyone ever had to.

My dogs share a common thread with Mr. Driscoll. He was as unaware that his simple words changed a life by giving it direction. And, as Scoshi sits over my shoulder on the sofa now, a perch that allows him to see out over the entire world, he has no idea the imprint our fifteen years together have had. He taught me to bark when necessary and to always bark the truth; to be grateful for every meal and every moment, and the abundance they represent. He taught me never to fear a face-off at the fence or miss a chance to nap. All I did in return was teach him a few tricks and how to drive a car.

Betty taught me that if you leap the net will appear, that when you wag your tail it makes everyone feel better, and that every moment has the potential to change your life. She's too busy shaking the life out of the Little Yellow Man right now to recall those lessons.

And so, too, have those who have passed on — Taffy, Ding, and now Reagan — had their place in my life. Taffy showed me that compassion is best expressed by listening. From Ding I learned to run with my heart, not my legs. Reagan taught me that when you learn that you are lovable, someone will always want to pet you.

I never had the chance to thank Mr. Driscoll personally, although I spoke about him in a speech I gave several years ago. An astute reporter in the audience picked up on my remarks and printed them in an article in the newspaper. That article found its way to Mr. Driscoll, who had long since left the Connecticut area for another school on Long Island. He wrote a touching note back to me, thanking me for the kind words about him in my speech. He recalled me as a student, but had no memory of his words of encouragement.

So I try not to make the same mistake with my dogs. They ask so little in return for what they give, yet they give so much, and they give in silence.

It causes me to pause and remember that line from the poem I wrote at sixteen:

I am of those I've touched, and the best of
what they are.

And I was right.

PHOTO CREDITS

ABOUT THE AUTHOR

Award-winning actor, host, composer, and writer — and lifelong dog lover — **John O'Hurley** is one of television's busiest and most versatile personalities. Since 2002, he has served as the host of NBC's National Dog Show presented by Purina®. In 2005, he danced his way into the hearts of America as the ultimate champion of the hit ABC show *Dancing with the Stars* — and was selected as one of *People* magazine's "sexiest men alive." He is well-known for his portrayal of the wry and witty J. Peterman on *Seinfeld,* and as the voice of popular cartoon characters, such as "King Neptune" in *SpongeBob SquarePants.* And in 2006, he made his Broadway debut as the lead male role of Billy Flynn, in *Chicago.* He currently hosts the widely syndicated game show classic *Family Feud.*

When he's not performing, John maintains his single-digit handicap by playing on the

Celebrity Players Tour and other charity tournaments. He lives in Los Angeles with his wife, Lisa, and their two dogs, Betty and Scoshi.

The employees of Thorndike Press hope you have enjoyed this Large Print book. All our Thorndike and Wheeler Large Print titles are designed for easy reading, and all our books are made to last. Other Thorndike Press Large Print books are available at your library, through selected bookstores, or directly from us.

For information about titles, please call:
(800) 223-1244

or visit our Web site at:
www.gale.com/thorndike
www.gale.com/wheeler

To share your comments, please write:
Publisher
Thorndike Press
295 Kennedy Memorial Drive
Waterville, ME 04901